POWERHOUSE

How to get out of your own way, fullfill your unique
purpose, and live a powerful life

LINDSEY SCHWARTZ

PEACOCK PROUD
P·R·E·S·S

Book Cover: Amelia Walsh, www.ameliawalsh.com

Portrait Photographer: Bree Cota, www.breemariephotography.org

Editor: Laura L. Bush

DISCLAIMER:
This is a work of nonfiction. The information is of a general nature to help readers know and understand more about their money. Readers of this publication agree that Lindsey Schwartz will not be held responsible or liable for damages that may be alleged or resulting directly or indirectly from their use of this publication. All external links are provided as a resource only and are not guaranteed to remain active for any length of time. The author cannot be held accountable for the information provided by, or actions resulting from accessing these resources.

For my incredible husband, Elliot.
Thank you for relentlessly seeing me as powerful and pouring
belief into my crazy dreams. I love you.

The most common way people give up their power is by thinking they don't have any.

--**Alice Walker**

Table of Contents

INTRODUCTION:
YOU ARE A POWERHOUSE

Powerhouse Woman: A woman of influence, high-vibe energy and strength, who uses her innate creative power for the greater good.

Do you feel called to fulfill a bigger purpose? Are you stuck in a career you don't love but afraid to start over from scratch? Is something tugging at your heart—a message that you want to share, a product that you want to create, or a revolutionary idea that will shape the future and impact countless lives? Are you paralyzed by fear or by not being able to articulate what you *really* want?

If so, this book is for you. And let me just start by saying, I *know* how you feel.

For the better part of five years, I felt stuck. Sure, I was happy, but I couldn't deny the feeling that there was something *more* for me. I started tuning in to that nagging tug at my heart and in doing so completely reinvented myself, creating a business and life beyond my wildest dreams. I went from feeling like I was slowly dying inside pursuing the corporate "dream" to starting my own part-time business on the side, eventually freeing myself from the 9-to-5 grind. I even doubled my income while simultaneously creating more freedom and fulfillment in all areas of my life. I share this personal history with you because all of it, and more, is available when you connect to your purpose and unapologetically work to bring your own dreams to life.

But why aren't more of us doing exactly that?

Women, by nature, are designed to create. The ability to generate human *life* is literally woven into our DNA. We all have this creative power in common, yet I think we also share many of the same blocks around fully stepping into it. I don't know about you, but I haven't always felt connected to my own power.

I've always been drawn to and inspired by strong women who unapologetically pursue their unique purpose and are on fire to create change in the world. Powerhouse women. Confidence, charisma, beauty, and strength—these were all traits that I could easily identify in others, but in me? I felt like the least likely candidate. I've always considered myself a high achiever, or at least that's what I had people fooled into thinking about me. I was on the honor roll, participated in every sport from softball to competitive cheerleading, had lots of friends, and never caused trouble. I carefully crafted my life to make it appear as though I had it all together. But it was all a mask, cleverly designed to cover up what I really didn't want people to know about me: I was scared. No. I was *petrified*—of everything.

Of not being good enough.

Of not being liked.

Of not meeting my own expectations.

I desperately sought out the approval of others so much that I didn't even know what I really stood for.

Do you ever feel like you're hiding behind a mask? Like you're afraid of people seeing you for who you really are? If there's one thing I've learned, it's nearly impossible to make the difference you're destined to make while disguising your authentic self. I've had to interrupt some deeply rooted habits and face my insecurities head-on to get to where I am today. And just when I think I've "arrived" at some new level of awesomeness, I realize how much more work there is for me to do.

Along the way to my own self-discovery, something radical occurred to me. What if, instead of working to *become* a total powerhouse like all the strong women I admired, I simply needed to get out of the way and let her shine through? What if all I had to do was unleash a part of me that *already existed*? This one simple realization changed everything. And that is what I intend for this book to help you do—reveal the power that already exists within you, so you can connect with your purpose and bring it to life. You don't have to work to *become* a powerhouse woman; it's who you *already are*, so let's unleash you.

Your individual expression of a powerhouse woman will be completely unique. No one else in the world will make an impact quite like you. Maybe you'll make your mark through business or a passion project that's tugging at your heart. Maybe you'll discover a cure, write a book, design beautiful buildings, or start a nonprofit. Maybe your greatest contribution will come through your role as a wife, mother, sister, or daughter. Maybe you'll be the next president— or maybe you're raising her. It's all equally valuable and vitally needed.

Just pause to think about this for a minute: how many world problems could we solve together as women if each of us stepped into our full potential and unleashed our inner power? How many lives could we impact? And what kind of example would we set for the next generation of women who are watching our every move? Every day, women just like you are making a deep and lasting impact on the world by tapping into their own unique expression of the creative genius we all possess. And there's plenty of room for you to join the party.

I'll relate the principles in this book specifically to creating a business or passion project, but the concepts apply regardless of your unique purpose. But let me be clear, this book will not tell you *how* to start or grow a business, or how to launch your passion project to the world. I won't tell you the exact steps to take in order to fulfill on your purpose. What this book will teach you is to leverage the power that is already within you—how to access the self-confidence that is always available, how to squash the ugly effects of comparison, how to loosen the death grip on your comfort zone so you can really fly, and how to leverage the power of your words to manifest results quickly. I can't wait to share everything I've learned (and am still learning) along my own path. If you're willing to do the work, you, too, can start to turn your brilliant ideas into reality and reconnect with the confident, courageous, and fierce woman you already are.

The principles I'll share are those that I apply in my own life daily. Some have taken me years to *begin* to master. I still have breakdowns. I'm constantly learning what it takes to go to the next level, and by no means do I have success all figured out. But when I was first starting out in my own self-discovery journey, I would have loved to know that there was someone else who felt the same fears that I did and overcame them to become successful anyway.

HOW TO GET THE MOST OUT OF THIS BOOK

Before we get started, it's important for me to let you in on a little secret. For any of the ideas or strategies I'll share to work for YOU, the first step is to accept responsibility that *you have a say in how your life goes*. The most basic principle underlying anything else I'll share with you is that you are completely responsible for your life. And I don't mean "responsible" as in *it's all your fault* if your life isn't already going the way you want it to. This isn't an invitation to host your own private pity party. You've done the best you can, given the tools you've had so far, and now you're going to learn some new tools.

Accepting responsibility and giving up all blame is a really powerful place to stand. It's a gift you give yourself because it means that you hold the power to change any outcome that you don't like.

Let me give you a preview of coming attractions so you can get a sense of the kind of work we'll do together. And yes, I said *work* ... as in, to have something different you'll have to do something different. That makes sense, right? Your thoughts, habits, and actions up to this point have produced the results you currently have, so if you want to take things to the next level or change course completely, you'll need to do something you've never done before. That's where the magic happens.

Regardless of whether you want a successful business, a healthy and fit body, or a happy relationship, the way you get there is the same—focus on learning to *become* the person who naturally produces the result you desire. Take action to build the *beliefs* and *habits* consistent with the outcome, and the beliefs and habits will produce the results naturally. Your entire paradigm changes, and you find yourself naturally waking up each day taking the actions consistent with your goals.

Everything we'll do from this point forward is aimed at breaking down any old beliefs or habits that no longer serve you and replacing them with those that do. I'll teach you everything I've learned about creating a mindset for success, leveraging the power of your thoughts and words, and creating productive habits that stick. Think of it all like building a muscle. As the muscle gets stronger, things start to flow, leaving you naturally able to rock your business or passion project with power, confidence, and ease. And I'm all about flow, baby.

If you're anything like me, this isn't the first book on success that you've picked up. I've read a lot of great books along the way, but none of them had a lasting impact until I consciously *applied* what I was reading in my life. The best way to ensure that you get everything you possibly can from this interactive guide is to dive in and play full out. Your book should look messy when you're done with it. Please write in it, mark the pages you want to revisit, and highlight your "aha!" moments.

I designed this book to help you tap into your innate creative power and show you that everything you need to live a powerhouse life is already within you. You'll notice that the book is divided into twelve sections, each focused on a different power that you already possess (although you may not be using it as designed). I recommend spending a full week diving into each power before moving on to the next. At the end of every chapter, you'll find a set of questions to help you deepen your understanding. Your answers, along with the Powerhouse Action Plan, will help you take what you've learned and apply it in your life, helping you reap the benefits of your practice right away. I designed the book this way for an important reason. You cannot implement everything all at once. Trying to do so would likely leave you overwhelmed and returning to old patterns. Look at this experience as a journey that will build on the previous lesson. Once you've completed all twelve chapters, you may even want to revisit and do more work on some of the concepts until you've mastered them.

MANAGING EXPECTATIONS

How long will it *really* take to fully unleash your own inner powerhouse woman? That's a great question. The answer is—as long as it takes. We live in an *I want it now world*. Sites like Amazon will deliver purchases in less than two hours. At the click of a mouse, we have digital access to music, books, and movies. Not a day goes by without the mention of a new quick-fix diet plan. Let's be honest. Digging in and doing the work, regardless of how long it takes, is not the easy route. I find myself wishing for a fast-forward button that would allow me to skip right to the end result, too. Maybe I could have found a faster way to produce the same results in my business, but would I have become the woman I am today? Probably not. And I wouldn't trade any amount of money for the lessons that have made me into the most confident, happy, fulfilled version of myself to date (and I'm fully expecting that as I keep moving forward, I'll discover new levels of even deeper fulfillment and joy). Let's get one thing straight—you can't microwave your way to lasting success.

So now let's talk about you. Have you been ignoring that nagging feeling that you'd rather be doing something other than what you're currently doing? Is there a passion project on your heart that you haven't made time to create? Do you want to reinvent yourself and start pursuing what makes your heart sing? Are you waiting for someone to anoint you as "ready" to be the world changer you already are?

Something tells me that if you picked up this book, you're looking for more—more freedom, excitement, contribution, a deeper sense of purpose, or perhaps "more" of something you haven't quite put your finger on yet. Am I right?

Well, sister, you can't hide anymore. I see you for who you really are, and you're ready.

If you were waiting for permission, this is it.

Let it rip and go for it! Why *not* you? Why *not* now? It's never too late to reinvent yourself and start pursuing what you're passionate about. Never. We live in an era where the opportunities for women are more abundant than ever, regardless of age, education, social status, or income—especially if you live in the developed world. I'm not saying that you won't face challenges, but there are countless stories of women who overcame incredible odds to achieve massive success in life. All it takes is a little courage to get started and a willingness to never quit.

If you're ready, then let's get started. Here's to changing the world and chasing your dreams in the cutest pair of shoes you own!

PART 1: CONNECT WITH YOUR PURPOSE

The powerhouse women I've admired always seem deeply connected to a purpose greater than themselves. I used to think that I couldn't step into my own full potential without clearly knowing what I was put on this earth to do. For a long time, I did nothing because I didn't know my exact purpose. Do you ever get caught in that trap too?

Here's what I've learned. Connecting with your purpose isn't a destination you reach; it's a lifelong adventure and a path that's constantly evolving. Give yourself permission to start somewhere, anywhere, and allow space for your interests and desires to evolve and change as you do. What you start out doing isn't likely to be the exact same thing you will be doing five or ten years from now. Sometimes you have to find out which things are NOT aligned with your purpose before you hone in on what really makes your heart sing.

In the next chapter, you'll look at the first power that you possess but may not be using as designed: the ability to identify the subtle clues from your soul that are trying to point you in the right direction.

POWER #1:
USE THE NUDGE AS YOUR GUIDE

Identifying and connecting with your unique purpose typically begins with a subtle nudge. This nudge can come in the form of an idea that makes your heart beat a little faster, a curiosity that you just can't shake, or a nagging feeling that there is more for you. Your nudge is like a subtle little love tap from your soul or the "poke" feature on Facebook (except this time it's not from a creeper). The nudge quietly asks for your attention, but it will not beg.

My guess is that if you picked up this book, you're well aware of your nudge and already on your way toward defining and bringing your vision to life. There's a lot for you to gain from our time together, but I want to dedicate these next few paragraphs to those of you who have a sense that you may have felt a nudge at some point, but you haven't fully diagnosed it yet. *I think I felt a nudge. Was that a nudge? Or was it just indigestion? How can I be sure that nudge was for me, and that I wasn't standing in the way of someone else's nudge?*

Rarely will your nudge appear in a flash of lightning or a Morgan Freeman voiceover from heaven. A nudge can be easy to overlook if life is too cluttered. It's often in a quiet moment that the nudge whispers *psst*. I think a lot of people feel these little love taps from their soul, but it takes a special kind of person to *accept* the adventure of pursuing a nudge. Someone like you.

If you're questioning whether or not that psst was your nudge—it was. Now, that doesn't mean you're required to *do* anything about it, but if you have ever experienced a passing thought of *maybe there is more . . .* you've been nudged. It may have startled you, or you're busy resisting it, or you're questioning whether it was really meant for you. If you're anything like me, acknowledging that there was, indeed, a nudge was the first and most unnerving part of the journey. Acknowledging the nudge meant you were now responsible for choosing to investigate it further or spend your entire life wondering *what if?*

Acknowledging your nudge takes courage because what to do with a nudge is almost never spelled out clearly. Some nudges emerge from a place of raw necessity. You hit rock bottom, and the nudge is your way out. Mine wasn't like that, which I think made it even more confronting in a way. My life was actually really great at the time. Still, I couldn't deny the feeling that I was meant for something *more*. I had to wrestle with an important question when I started to feel a nudge toward more—is it *really* ok to be totally happy and at the same time want more? Is it *really* ok to be grateful for what I already have and see a bigger calling?

Growing up in the Midwest, my family didn't have a lot in terms of financial wealth, but what we lacked in money, we made up for big time in love and happiness. My childhood was filled with the most beautiful memories and experiences—all before Candy Crush, the iPad, or Netflix. As a kid, I had no idea how much my mom was stretching every dollar and finding creative ways to entertain us. I never once felt I was missing out on anything. A sense of contentment for what we had was woven into the fabric of our family, so as an adult, when I first started to feel a subtle love tap that there was *more* for me, I ignored it.

My nudge came not long after I started my first job out of college. I was about a year into my corporate career, and on paper you could say I had a pretty sweet gig for a twenty-something young woman. I was recruited by a large company to work in outside sales for their commercial division. They paid all the moving expenses for me to relocate to Arizona, a place where it doesn't snow. (Growing up in the Midwest, this alone was like hitting the lottery.) I had a company car, cell phone, and expense account. I had a great boss and coworkers, the ability to work from home, and I could set my own schedule. But a year in, I was very clear that this career path was **not** for me forever. I couldn't put my finger on exactly why I knew, but something was off. I wrestled for a while feeling that I should just be grateful for the position I had, especially since my nudge occurred during a severe economic downturn when I watched dozens of my friends get laid off and have trouble finding work. There I was, with a stable career in an extremely unstable and scary economic environment. But I wanted out.

The nudge, as it turns out, cares nothing about visiting at a convenient time and for good reason:

Your nudge is not about you.

The kind of nudge I'm talking about isn't inherently driven by a self-serving need or the desire to be rich and famous (although money may be a necessary tool to help you reach more people). Your nudge is 100 percent about who you are going to *serve*. You wouldn't be nudged into action unless there was a request from humanity that needed to be filled. If you've been nudged, someone out there *wants and needs what you have to offer*. The degree of financial success, acknowledgement, and personal fulfillment you achieve along the way will be a direct reflection of how many lives you impact.

So back to the question—is it *really* ok to be totally happy and at the same time want more? Yes! Hell, yes! In fact, being grateful for what you have while remaining open to more abundance, contribution, and fulfillment is the sweet spot. But if you notice yourself wrestling with the question like I did, consider that it may be a clever distraction to keep you from taking responsibility for the impact you know you're meant to make. Being grateful for what you already have actually makes you the perfect candidate for a nudge. If you're not deeply grateful for what you already have, how can you expect to be entrusted with more?

There are all sorts of creative ways we resist taking action on our nudge. I don't think we're ever nudged to do something we already know how to do. Otherwise we'd already be doing it. A nudge, therefore, is an invitation to *grow*. So if the mere thought of your nudge feels scary and uncomfortable, you're exactly where you should be. If you're not right now pursuing your unique nudge, or you're at a point in the journey where you feel stuck, chances are you're just ready to grow to the next level. It doesn't mean the nudge is no longer for you or you've failed to bring it to life. Doing the inner work to become the person who will bring the vision behind your nudge to life only deepens the massive contribution you will make.

BREAD CRUMBS

If the most confronting part of the journey is acknowledging the nudge and choosing to pursue it, I think the hardest part is getting started. I admit, I'm a little Type A. Okay, a lot Type A. I don't particularly like starting a pursuit when I don't know the end result and can't clearly see steps one through one thousand. I know, I'm a real party animal. In my experience, pursuing a nudge is a little bit like walking forward into thick fog. You may only be able to see the next one or two steps in front of you. Call me crazy, but I've seen one too many horror movies involving dark foggy nights, so stepping forward into the unknown can be scary enough to make a grown woman cry (and by grown woman, I mean me).

But here's what I've started to realize. When pursuing your nudge, the goal isn't to know exactly where you'll end up; the goal is simply to figure out where to *start*. I don't think there's really an "end" to the pursuit of your nudge, and there isn't just one singular purpose for you. Life is more about going from one nudge to the next, following your curiosities like a trail of bread crumbs, and paying close attention to the directions your inner guide gives you along the way. The path almost always looks more like a curly straw than a straight line. Just ask any five-year-old. Curly straws are always more fun.

When my nudge came calling, I wasn't immediately sure what to do with it, but I started to become acutely aware of the fact that some people are paid a LOT of money to do things that others do for fun. For example, my dad loves golf. He can't wait for his vacation time each year so he can spend more time on the golf course. On the other hand, professional golfers are paid a lot of money to golf year round. They are *paid* to do what others do for fun. I certainly wasn't about to become a professional athlete overnight (nor did I want to), so I went in search of my own answer to the question—*what would I love to do, whether or not I was being paid for it?*

I wish I could say that I initially had some huge vision to impact the world, but I couldn't see that far yet. I didn't want just another job, and I had never really thought about what I would *love* to do. There are a lot of things that I could make a good living doing, but what's the point of climbing the ladder of success only to realize it's leaning against the wrong wall? All I could see was that the corporate dream I had chased wasn't for me anymore. That realization led me to the first bread crumb on the trail . . . answering the simple question of well, what would I love to do?

I didn't have a clear answer to the question at first, but what I kept coming back to was fairly simple. The thing I would do every day, whether I was being paid to do it or not, revolved around health and fitness. I was already devoting a chunk of time every day to my own health and fitness routine, and I wasn't being paid for it. So why *not* create a life where I'm paid to be the healthiest version of myself and use that as a platform to inspire others? That simple idea is where my journey started. From there, my own journey has evolved into something far bigger than I could've imagined.

Your own curiosities and interests are bread crumbs for your journey too. Pursuing your curiosities is a great place to start in connecting with your purpose.

Did you ever read those *Choose Your Own Adventure* books as a kid? Those books were my jam. I was written into the story as the main character, and every choice I made led me down a different path, some with a hero's ending and others with a fiery death. If I didn't like the ending I chose, I could always backtrack and try another path because, hey . . . it was just a made-up story, anyway. I think pursuing your nudge is kind of like that, and you'd do yourself a huge favor if you'd relax a bit and realize that at any moment you can choose to try a new path.

I've probably tried more avenues that didn't pan out along the way than those that did. And I wouldn't change a thing because each twist and turn taught me something. I love looking back at all the pieces that had to line up in order for me to get to where I am today. Have you ever reflected back on your own trail of bread crumbs like that? One simple choice that led to another, one seemingly insignificant meeting that opened a door, or one brave moment when you stepped out of your comfort zone, and your whole future shifted. It's fun to connect the dots, isn't it? I choose to believe it's all divinely connected. All of it is perfectly orchestrated in your favor, even when it doesn't seem so in the moment. *Especially* when it doesn't seem like things are going your way. Hey, I get to choose my own adventure right? The context I create for my life's adventure is all made up anyway, so I consciously choose a context that inspires me. And you can, too.

When I first acknowledged my nudge, I didn't immediately resign from my job, even though for me, that was the end goal. Resigning too early would have added unnecessary stress that could very well have suffocated my nudge altogether. Instead I started small, with one step in the direction of my curiosity—health and fitness. First I got certified to teach spin class (something I loved) and picked up one class a week at a small local gym. It was the only place that would hire me, so I took the job. We can't always choose where the trail of bread crumbs starts. There was no instructor microphone, so I had to shout over the loud thumping music every class. The spin bikes were old and would constantly break down. Over the next year, I probably spent more money in gas driving to and from the gym than the twenty dollars I was paid to teach each week. Eventually, I came to realize that I liked being a participant in spin class more than I liked being an instructor, so I quit. On to the next bread crumb.

During my year teaching spin, I had also partnered with a nutrition company in the network marketing industry and started my own business part time, which is by far one of the best decisions I've ever made. Any business structure that allows you to leverage your time and involves minimal risk and financial investment to get started is always a great thing. In this company (where I still have a thriving business today), the culture of personal development and the opportunity of residual income provided the perfect environment for me to work steadily toward replacing my full-time income, all while transforming myself and learning how to run a business. It took me a little over two years to replace the income I was earning in my corporate job. At that point, my husband and I decided that I would resign from my job to pursue the business full time. That freed up more time and energy to pursue other curiosities, but it's definitely not where the trail of bread crumbs ends.

In the process of growing my network marketing business, I started to see other athletes using the same nutrition program I was using and having success in the arena of fitness competitions. Bam! Next breadcrumb. I had always been curious about competing in fitness anyway (curiosity = breadcrumb), so I thought *why not me?* I've always been active but had never taken my body to an elite level of fitness. This bread crumb was going to involve some seriously sore muscles and a whole new mindset around food.

I pushed my mind and body to new limits, and in the process learned that I am capable of far more than I give myself credit for. Over the next three years, I competed in seven fitness shows. Athletes like me from around the world were judged on our overall lean muscle tone, body symmetry, and stage presence. Walking across a stage wearing a sparkly bikini and six-inch high heels with a spray tan that would rival the cast of *Jersey Shore* might sound like an odd place to experience a new sense of personal empowerment, but the experience felt unbelievably transformative. Stepping into the fitness world showed me that I could reinvent myself at any moment I choose. As soon as the blinged-out bikini and glowing spray tan went on, I transformed into my alter ego. I may not have felt powerful or confident in my day-to-day life, but onstage, I channeled the persona of all the powerhouse women I admired.

Taking home the title of Miss Bikini Arizona two years in a row, I experienced great success in the fitness competition world. My achievements gave me a new platform to impact people in health and wellness. On the surface, it seemed like the perfect avenue to grow my nutrition business. I've come to realize, though, that some bread crumbs are just a stepping stone to prepare me (and you) for the next part of our journey. As I started to build a brand for myself in fitness, I felt nudged toward a slightly different direction—helping women connect with their inner power.

The book you're holding right now is my current bread crumb. Where will it lead? I don't know! I'll just keep following my intuition, my curiosities, and my truth. The point is this: I never knew that answering the simple question of "What would I love to do?" would lead me to this point. I couldn't have planned it if I'd tried. And when I started, I wasn't ready for the bread crumb I'm currently chasing. I had to undergo some major growth before I felt ready to deliver this message to you. Every twist and turn, every stale or moldy bread crumb that didn't pan out, was perfectly placed and part of my adventure for a reason.

My biggest takeaway from this chapter:

I'm doing exactly the right thing!
I'm following my nudge. and it's
bringing me joy.

LET'S RECAP

- Connecting with your purpose often begins with a subtle nudge—an idea that makes your heart beat a little faster, a curiosity that you just can't shake, or a nagging feeling that there is more for you.
- Your nudge is not about you. It's 100 percent about who you are going to serve.
- The goal of your nudge isn't to clearly identify your purpose from start to finish. The goal is just to figure out where to start.
- Pursuing your nudge will often feel scary and uncomfortable because a nudge is an invitation to grow.
- Your curiosities are clues to help you connect with your bigger purpose. Follow them.

POWERHOUSE ACTION PLAN:
FOLLOW THE NUDGE

Your challenge this week is to dig a little deeper into your nudge by answering four key questions below. Spend some time journaling about your answers. See if you can identify a new curiosity or new avenue in pursuing your nudge that you hadn't considered before. Remember, the goal isn't to be crystal clear on your big purpose. Your only goal is to identify one or two of the next steps you could try. Write down anything and everything that comes to mind as you reflect on these questions. There are no right answers. You may have to write through some superficial fluff before you get to the juicy stuff. Even if you think you're crystal clear about your purpose, reviewing these questions on an ongoing basis may reveal a deeper calling that you aren't conscious of right now.

Question 1: How do I want to *feel?*

I love setting goals. And if I'm not careful, I get too focused on the end result and don't allow myself to experience the fulfillment of having reached a particular goal. One of the biggest lessons I've learned is that it's not actually results we're after. It's the *feeling* that we believe those results will give us. Think about it. If you have a goal to lose 10 pounds, it's not the number on the scale that you are really after, but how you believe that number will make you feel. If you get clear about the core feelings you want to experience and stay open to the pathway that will lead to the feelings, you are more likely to come up with creative options that you may not have considered otherwise. Identifying the feelings you want to experience along the way in pursuit of your nudge is also a

great way to check in with yourself and make sure you're on track.
I want to feel:

fulfilled   joyful
energetic
free   happy
peaceful

loving

Once you've identified how you want to feel on a daily basis, here's the best part—there is no need to wait until you've arrived at a certain point in your journey to start feeling the way you want to feel. I've found that the more I can find small ways to start experiencing more of my desired feelings *now*, the faster my goals become a reality. For example, if one of my deepest desires is to feel creative or inspired, I'll ask myself, "What can I do today to experience that feeling?" It might be to take a walk in nature, to draw, to meditate, or have a spontaneous dance party in the middle of my kitchen.

List three things that you can do immediately to help you start feeling more of your top three desired feelings (Bonus points if you plan one of these activities in your calendar this week!):

1. journal / write an intention for the week

2. read for pleasure

3. help someone feel good about himself/herself

Question 2: What can I teach people, or how can I serve others?

We all have at least one thing that we're uniquely equipped to contribute, and I believe that one fast track to unleashing your inner powerhouse is through serving others. As Zig Ziglar, the author and motivational speaker, put it, "You can have everything in life you want if you will just help other people get what they want." What unique gifts do you have? What has your life experience taught you? What knowledge have you gained that others are seeking? How can you use your story to give someone else hope?

Don't discount any of your life experience or think your journey isn't significant enough to make a difference. The most beautiful gift you can offer in service to others is the most authentic version of yourself, flaws and all. What struggles have you faced and how are you overcoming them? One way to start making a difference is to give a voice to a particular struggle you may be facing, so that others in the same position know that they aren't alone. You don't have to have anything "handled" before you can start making a difference. You're most relatable when you are *on the journey* yourself. What are some creative ways you can share your journey along the way and inspire others?

What do other people want to learn that you already know? What are the top three questions you are always being asked ?

1. handling death of a spouse
2. kids / advice on kids
3. organization
4. living the dream

Question 3: What makes me sad/mad/happy? What excites me most?

What worthy cause breaks your heart, or what social injustice do you want to impact? Some of the most successful business ventures and philanthropic endeavors came out of a simple desire to solve a problem that no one else was solving. Even if your business or passion project doesn't solely exist to tackle social issues, maybe you create a service component where every sale you make contributes to a cause you're passionate about. It's no coincidence that some of the most successful businesses are also the most generous.

On the flip side, what makes you happiest or what do you enjoy doing more than anything in the world? How can you incorporate more of that into your business or passion project? Maybe you love being in nature, but your business is run out of an office or your home. You could plan a retreat for your team—a time for all of you to unplug from technology and connect with each other to discuss ideas and dreams for the future. It can be tempting, especially in the early stages of a new venture, to be all work all the time. Don't get me wrong, launching a new project absolutely requires you to grind it out. But the more you fill your love cup with things and experiences that light you up, the more that relaxed positive energy will permeate into your business and those you impact.

> yes!

What excites me:

When I'm teaching someone something and they "get it"

What makes me happiest:

- helping others help themselves
- speaking Spanish

Causes I'm passionate about:

helping young adults w/ addiction

One creative way I can incorporate the above into my weekly routine:

Question 4: What does my ideal day look like?

Imagine yourself as a powerhouse woman fully living her purpose. What do you see? Are you sitting in a beautifully furnished office or working from your laptop overlooking the ocean? Are you working around people or flying solo? What kind of people are you interacting with? Are they positive and uplifting? Is your typical work day wardrobe a fab business suit with pointy stilettos, yoga pants with your hair in a topknot, or a mix of everything in between?

Painting the picture down to the minute detail and engaging all of your senses is a powerful way to speed up the process of creating your dream life. What are the smells, sounds, and emotions you're experiencing? See yourself walking through your ideal day fulfilled, happy, and on purpose. The more vivid the picture in your mind, the faster it will manifest into reality.

Describe your ideal day from start to finish. The more vivid the details, the better!

I wake up because my body is ready. I feel rested and excited to start my day. I'm so pumped to get going an see what good things come today. Good things have been consistantly coming to me since I began this journey. All these cool people bringing cool vibes and energy into the world. My tribe is changing the world! This journey began with a, "Why not?!" and it's exploded ever since. I knew this would happen - that I'd be sitting here drinking my hot morning beverage in this kick-ass house while looking out at this stunning view of Puget Sound. I just never imagined it would happen so QUICKLY!

You may not be 100 percent clear on your answers to the above questions, and that's okay too. Start by digging deeper into what you are most curious about. Don't judge anything you come up with or think any answer is too farfetched or silly. You won't get what you don't ask for. This is the time to be bold, honest, and let yourself dream.

Before we move forward, I have one final question: **What is stopping you from pursuing your nudge or slowing your progress? What gets in your way?**

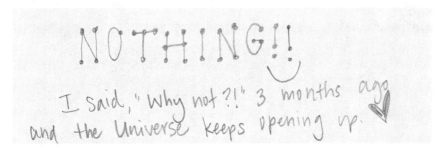

NOTHING!!

I said, "Why not?!" 3 months ago and the Universe keeps opening up.

I would bet some of your answers are the same things I said to myself and that kept me from getting started: *I don't have any skills or a degree in that area. Why would anyone listen to ME? Someone else is already doing what I want to do and doing it better. I'm too young. I'm too old. I don't have enough time. I don't have enough money. What if I fail? What if I succeed? I don't know if I can handle the responsibility of all of those people counting on me . . .*

My own lack of confidence, fear of failure, and ironically, my fear of success were paralyzing at times. Throughout our time together, I'll share what I've learned about harnessing the power of mindset and language to karate chop through my own limiting beliefs. I'll also share insight into how I'm now able to take action in spite of the fear. I've been blessed to create success in areas that I could've only dreamed about when I first said yes to my nudge, yet I still don't have it all figured out and probably never will. I don't know if the fears of failure and success ever truly go away. This may sound crazy, but I don't think I would want my fears to fade entirely. They keep me humble, and they keep me hungry.

Any time I grow to the next level in my business or life, there are always a few habits (and even sometimes a few people) that don't come with me. They can't come with me if I'm going to go where I need to go. The same goes for you and your nudge. Before you can fully unleash your inner powerhouse and build a new foundation for your own success, it's vitally important to examine and break up with any beliefs and habits that no longer serve you.

PART 2: THE BREAK UP

Have you ever been in a relationship that you *know* isn't right, but you let it go on far past its expiration date? If you have, I'm sure your reasons for doing so were similar to mine. *It's comfortable. I should try to make it work. It's really not that bad. I don't want to hurt feelings. I'm afraid of being alone.* It's like in some weird masochistic way we'd rather put up with the dull pain of staying in a relationship we know is over than deal with the temporary pain of ending it. Crazy, right?

Yet we do the *same* thing with some of our limiting beliefs and habits. You know, the ones that keep you stuck, dim your bright shiny light, and have you play small. The ones that have you disconnect from the powerhouse woman you truly are. But not anymore. It's time to end things for good with the beliefs and habits that no longer serve you. And no, we don't have to let them down gently with any of that *"It's not you. It's me"* B.S. Sorry, habits. It's you. It's definitely you.

I'm sure we each have our own laundry list of persistent crappy beliefs and habits that need to go, but let's keep it simple and start with three that I believe are the root cause of all others: the three C's—confidence, comparison, and comfort. They are all interconnected, and, together, they form the perfect cocktail of self-sabotage, self-doubt, and insecurity. That's certainly not a cocktail I would order at happy hour.

This breakup isn't for your own selfish benefit—it's for the countless lives that you are going to impact. We'll devote the next three lessons to looking closely at the impact that the three C's are having in your life. Breakups are never easy, so we'll do this together. I'll bring the tissues and a tub of cookie dough ice cream just in case.

POWER #2:
UNLOCK YOUR INNER CONFIDENCE

Why is it that some nudges are brought to life while others never travel beyond the confines of our mind? What's the difference between the people who jump into action and those who spend their lives *thinking* about taking action? I wonder how many brilliant ideas end up in the landfill of unfulfilled nudges along with our old Barbie dolls and retainers, cast away because they appear to be of no use anymore. Maybe some of your own ideas have wound up at the dump. In reality, a nudge doesn't have an expiration date, so what has us sabotage a perfectly good idea? What gets in the way?

I bet that if we examined every unfulfilled nudge, we could boil down the primary saboteur into one common denominator—confidence. More specifically, broken confidence. Life happens, and your once whole and healthy self-confidence starts to develop tiny cracks. If not tended to, these cracks can expand, creating a giant canyon separating you from your goals and from the difference you are meant to make.

What do the cracks in your own confidence look like? Maybe your world has been rocked by an illness, the death of someone you love, a business failure, or the end of an important relationship. It might feel like your confidence has been replaced with doubt, fear, insecurity, or sadness. Maybe you operate in a state of high confidence most of the time, but whenever you go to swing out beyond your comfort zone, you experience paralyzing self-doubt. Maybe you hide your crazy big dreams and never share them with anyone. Instead, you settle for a smaller, pared-down goal that you know you can achieve. Or you might find yourself operating in overwhelm, chaos, or procrastination, all to cover up the cracks in your self-confidence. If you're anything like me, you're probably checking the box for "D, all of the above."

I truly believe that we always have access to confidence, although I'm the first to admit that isn't always what I experience. It's easy for the cracks in your confidence to start feeling "normal," when maybe you've just developed some bad habits that are blocking your access to the ever-present confidence that exists within you, my fellow powerhouse. It's there. I promise.

THE SELF-CONFIDENCE ROLLER COASTER

Self-confidence is a minefield, isn't it? One moment I'm on top of my game, strutting through my day as though the soundtrack to my life is Alicia Keys singing, "*This girl is on fiyaaa*," and the next I'm looking for the nearest rock to crawl under, painfully aware of my own doubts and insecurities. This roller coaster of high and low self-confidence seems to be especially magnified whenever I'm working toward a really big goal or doing something I've never done before. Do you ever notice that?

Pause here and answer this question—**where in your life right now is your confidence being tested most?**

Can I sustain this energy, this flow?

Really take some time to think about your answer. Doing so will help you to get the most out of this chapter. Is your confidence being tested most in starting your business or passion project and getting your message out? Reinventing yourself and starting over in a new industry? Learning a new skill or mastering a new technology? Jumping back into the dating pool? Or maybe you're stuck in that dreaded phase of *I don't know what the F to do next.*

For me, writing this book bought me a front-row seat on the scariest roller coaster my confidence has ridden to date—the kind that flips you upside down and holds you by the ankles while careening down a ninety-degree dive headfirst into a dark scary cave filled with bats. And circus clowns. And a dentist waiting to give you a root canal. That kind of roller coaster. Yeah, my confidence has been on quite the wild ride as of late.

To say that I never planned on writing a book is an understatement. I don't even *like* writing (or so I thought). I created a blog site several years ago and published one new article per *year.* Safe to say, I wasn't exactly cranking out hot content, nor did I really want to. Yet when the nudge for this book came calling, I couldn't deny the no-brainer opportunity of it, despite all the reasons my mind also came up with for not following through with it: *I don't have the time. I've never done it before. I'm not a writer. I don't know what to write about. It's all been said before.* Each reason was a desperate attempt to distract me from the real and raw questions underneath all my understandable fear— can I *really* do this? Will anyone care what I have to say?

The truth is, deep down I truly wanted to make a difference, and I knew writing a book could help me do that. As humans, if we're being honest, I think we all want to make a difference. Eventually, despite all my reasons for not writing a book, I realized I wanted to share my challenges and experiences in the hope that my story—both the struggles and the success—might help someone else in a similar situation. It turns out that it wasn't actually writing that I didn't like; it was putting myself out there and risking another person's judgment that I feared most. I was far too concerned about what people would think to even take the first step. By the way, this is not at all a new pattern in my life. It's funny how your mind always knows the perfect trump card to play in order to stop you from stepping out of your comfort zone. In fact, the moment I said yes to pursuing the nudge and writing this book, an epic tug of war between my nudge and my old self ensued. Even after I was well into the writing process, I felt torn between my comfort zone of pleasing others and staying small and the thrill of accomplishing something new and surprising myself. Cue the confidence roller coaster.

Obviously, since you're holding the book, this isn't a huge spoiler—I did finish writing it. And my confidence got a major workout in the process. Some days I sat at my desk for hours, managing to squeak out just a few paragraphs. Other days the inspiration flowed like a high-pressure hose; I could barely capture the thoughts and get them down on paper fast enough. And then there was the constant self-judgment. Just *thinking* about someone actually reading this book and judging and assessing what I've written sometimes made me short of breath, like a ten-ton elephant was sitting on my chest. I don't know about you, but my imagination works overtime dreaming up worst-case scenarios and playing them out on the big screen of my mind. I often sit there enjoying some buttery popcorn and watching the drama in my mind unfold, not realizing that I hold the remote control and can change the channel any time I want.

So if you currently feel like you are riding the confidence roller coaster too, you're in great company. That's what it feels like to pursue a goal that's bigger than yourself: wobbly knees, butterflies in your stomach, and sometimes feeling like you're gonna puke. The only way to avoid the ride is to not get on it at all, to play small and avoid all risk. But I'm guessing that's not why you're here. You know that you are being called to something bigger, so you may as well throw your hands in the air, let out your best tween girl scream and enjoy the ride. A level of uncertainty will always exist when you're working toward something you've never done before.

It's uncomfortable, downright scary at times, and *that's exactly how growth is supposed to feel.*

The ups and downs are inevitable, but here is the good news: confidence is like a muscle. You can build it so that eventually your confidence highs are even higher, and your low points are where the highs are now.

BUILDING YOUR CONFIDENCE MUSCLE

So if we all really do have access to confidence at any time, how do you tap into yours? And how can you strengthen or repair it when your confidence starts to develop cracks? To answer that, let's first have a look at four of the worst habits around confidence that I would guess most of us battle. Just like it would be a bad idea to build a beautiful new house on top of a faulty foundation, you can't build new habits on top of old crappy ones. Your existing beliefs, thought patterns, and habits are your foundation. When your foundation is solid, feeling confident will follow naturally.

After taking a closer look at each of the following crappy habits, you'll answer a few questions to help you identify how the habit shows up in your life and the impact it may be having on your confidence. After dissecting all four of these habits that undermine your confidence, we'll get to your action plan for this lesson and work together to build a stronger, more confident YOU in their place.

Crappy Habit #1: Inaction

We all have areas of life where we experience a higher level of confidence than others. Maybe it's in your career, or in your role as a mom/wife/sister/daughter/friend, or in playing an instrument or a sport. Maybe you make a mean pistachio cake like my BFF Jenna. Whatever it is, you can practically do it with your eyes closed.

How did you gain confidence in that area? And how long did it take? Even if you were born a child prodigy, my guess is that you had to put in the effort to gain the level of confidence you now have. You took the necessary actions, repeated over time, to achieve a certain level of mastery. You may have been uncomfortable at times, or even failed in some way, but that didn't deter you from moving forward and gaining confidence in your capability.

The really important lesson in looking at the areas where you've earned a higher level of confidence is this:

the *only* way to build more confidence in any area is by taking action.

I know, that doesn't sound like groundbreaking information. I hope you weren't looking for a big trade secret or something that wasn't already kind of obvious. See, I think deep down we all know that taking action produces results, and results produce confidence. But knowing and doing are two very different things. I'll be the first to admit that knowing did very little to help me break up with my paralyzing habits of inaction.

I want to give you and I some credit here. I'll bet there are a lot of areas where we're already taking action. But I'll invite you to check in (something I have to do all the time) and ask yourself, am I taking the right *kind* of action to move forward? I'm often guilty of keeping myself "busy" in order to avoid doing the things that are uncomfortable. And the things you are resisting, the actions that feel uncomfortable, are often exactly the actions needed to move you forward.

I learned through the process of writing this book that pressing *into* whatever it is I'm resisting is one of the best ways to develop confidence. So, on the days when writing felt challenging—like I was trying to move forward through thick mud—I still sat down and wrote for at least 15 minutes. I did the exact thing I was resisting. Sometimes I ended up scrapping everything I wrote; other days that 15 minutes turned into two hours because all I needed was a little push to get the ideas flowing. Little by little, the book started to come together. And slowly but surely, I started to find my voice. I started to *enjoy* writing. What I didn't expect is how much more inspired and creative I would feel in every area of my life as a result; and I never would have experienced that had I stopped taking action the moment I felt resistance.

This lesson is vital to remember when launching or growing a new business or project. I've seen incredibly talented people give up on their dream far too early because something was new and uncomfortable, never giving themselves the opportunity to earn the confidence they desired. Action is such a vital part of you bringing your nudge to life that we'll dedicate a whole section to it later on.

So what about you? Where are you resisting action? And what's stopping you from taking the next step in pursuit of your nudge? Take a few minutes to journal your thoughts. Don't judge anything that comes up; just write freely. Sometimes my best answers come out after I've gone through the more obvious ones. You may even experience resistance to doing this very exercise—it's all perfect! This is an opportunity to work through it and discover something new.

What are the three top actions I need to take in order to move my business or passion project forward?

1. ask my family (Mom, Dad, Kristi, Dick) to join me

2. keep putting myself out there & talking about it

3. meet w/ my leaders

What action(s) am I resisting?

1. ?

What actions do I use as an excuse to stay busy, but avoid the actions I really need to take? *Examples: social media, cleaning my house or office, taking unscheduled phone calls/meetings, etc.*

> I resist asking them because it feels super uncomfortable. I don't want to be judged. I don't mind them saying no to trying Isagenix. I mind being judged

What might be waiting for me on the other side of taking action? On the other side of resistance? *Examples: more confidence, inspiration, a greater impact on others, more happiness, etc.*

> Maybe they'll say yes! And if they do, these products could literally change their lives!

Crappy Habit #2: What You Say to Yourself, About Yourself

Building confidence around a new skill is one thing, but what about when your core confidence—the deep-rooted belief in yourself and your capability—gets damaged? How can you rebuild or strengthen it?

The first and most important place to look is at what you say *to* yourself *about* yourself. There is an inner critic inside you, constantly judging and assessing *everything*. You know, that voice that tells you how "not good enough" you are? Yeah, that's not God talking. This inner critic has an opinion about everything. And she isn't always your biggest fan. She knows all of your worst fears, your biggest mistakes, and your deepest insecurities—and she's not afraid to point them out. It's like a one-woman scene straight out of the movie *Mean Girls*, except you're playing the role of both the bully and the victim.

Be honest—if a friend said to your face half of the garbage you say to yourself, would you actually keep that person in your life? Probably not. Unless you enjoy misery.

There are two problems with this inner critic. The first is that she is present all day, every day. She follows wherever you go, and she's waiting to catch you in a moment of weakness. You can't get rid of her, so your only option is to turn down her microphone. The second, and most deadly problem, is that you often relate to her opinions as though they are the truth. You don't challenge what she says based on what it truly is—an opinion—but instead, you slip into her judgments like you're putting on a fur coat (faux fur, of course). Then you refuse to take the coat off when the summer temps hit, and you're no longer dressed for the occasion. If you are going to grow to the next level and make the impact you're out to make, it's time to reevaluate your wardrobe. And no, I'm not talking about the clothes hanging in your closet.

It's time to evaluate how many of your inner critic's judgments you've allowed to take up precious real estate in the closet of your mind.

How do you turn down the mic on this inner critic or at least lessen the grip of her running commentary has on your life? Well, for starters, you may have noticed that I refer to her in the third person. In other words, I choose to identify that "noise" as another person separate from myself. Now, before you turn me in to the nearest mental health facility, hear me out. I've learned that any destructive thoughts I'm thinking are not really coming from me, at least not the highest version of myself that I'm committed to becoming. I practice distinguishing and separating out any thoughts that aren't moving me forward from the thoughts that come from my true self, my true purpose. This gives me space to evaluate whether or not my inner critic's snarky opinions actually work for me or not. And she never stands on the sidelines with pom-poms shouting, "You can do it! I believe in you!"

The second way to silence your inner critic is to change her script. That's right; she's reading everything she says directly from a script. Here's the twisted thing: you wrote every word of that script. And the real shocker? *The script is all made up.* One hundred percent make-believe. It's as real as your favorite Disney princess. Now, you've been listening to your inner critic for much of your life, so it's not surprising that what she says *seems* real. But, hey, at one point in history, the earth was also flat, until it wasn't. That idea changed when someone thought to challenge what everyone believed to be true.

What if you were to challenge what you know to be "true" about yourself? What if you had the power to rewrite any of these "truths" that don't align with your vision for yourself and your life? Which ones would you choose to rewrite? *I'm shy. I don't know how to do that. I'm not smart enough. I'm not a writer. I'm not a singer. I'm not a salesperson. I don't like heights. I'm not a leader. I'm afraid of change. I need to see immediate results, or I'll give up. I'm not a strong speaker. I'm not an athlete. I'm an introvert.*

I'm jumping ahead a bit because we'll dive a lot deeper into the power of language later on, but this is very relevant to your self-confidence, so I can't skip over it. You unintentionally keep the self-confidence cracks in existence by reinforcing them with language—by what you say to yourself about yourself. It's all done out of habit, and most of it comes from your past:

- Someone calls you a name on the playground, and you make up that you're not liked. *I'll never be good enough.*
- You raise your hand to answer the teacher's question in first grade, but your answer is wrong and the entire class laughs. What do you decide in that moment? *I'm stupid.*
- You catch your first boyfriend holding hands with the most popular girl at school in the lunchroom. *I'm ugly. No one will ever love me.*
- Your marriage or business fails, and your confidence gets rocked along with it. *I'm a failure. I'm not worthy of love/success.*

Throughout your life, it's like your inner critic has followed closely behind you with a Fisher Price tape recorder, carefully documenting your "truths." She has a reeeaaaaaal Barbara Walters complex, this chick. Instead of writing off your self-judgments as something that was said in a moment of weakness, your inner critic adds them to the script and plays every word on repeat, even when the information is outdated and no longer relevant to your life. She's still playing cassette tapes, even though she's long overdue for an MP3 upgrade. Your internal negative chatter becomes the environment you walk around in all day long. No wonder your confidence has taken a hit. But wait . . . there's hope. Change what you say to yourself (even if it feels like a lie at first), and over time, you'll slowly begin to change the results in your life and business. We'll go a lot deeper into this shift later.

I wish that breaking up with the negative self-talk habit and developing confidence were as easy as popping in a new tape, but it takes time to hardwire your mind for something different. The second half of this book will be devoted to creating a new foundation for your confidence, success, and happiness. But for now, let's look at how crappy habit #2, your inner critic, may be affecting your confidence by answering these questions:

If you were to put your inner critic on loudspeaker, what are some of the negative things she says are "true" about you? *Examples: I'm not good enough. I'm stupid. No one likes me. I'll never be successful.*

If I could rewrite any of the "truths" I've decided about myself, what would they be?

Why am I committed to rewriting these "truths"? What would life be like if I were free from these limiting beliefs about myself?

Crappy Habit #3: Looking for Validation

This next habit is the ugly stepsister of negative self-talk. Whenever I'm not taking responsibility for the way I talk about myself to myself, it often leaves a gaping hole in my confidence. And in an effort to fill the void as quickly as possible, I've often looked to other people and things to validate me. Do you ever do the same? I'm sure we all have our own version of this habit. You take the "stable" job that you loathe because it's what your parents want you to do.

You stay in the friendship or romantic relationship that's draining you because it fulfills your desire to be needed. You take a thousand selfies, trying to find the perfect angle and lighting to maximize the number of likes you'll get when you post it. Or maybe you even turn to really unhealthy habits like drugs or alcohol to numb the pain and fill the void.

Now, there is nothing inherently wrong with doing some of these things. I'm all for a good selfie once in a while, and I love seeing yours. But when the motivation behind it is to fill a confidence void, that's where we go awry. Here's what I know to be true. No romantic relationship, number of "likes" on Facebook, or approval from another person can ever replace the feeling of pure self-acceptance and love. If you're going to break the habit of seeking outside validation and take back your confidence,

it's time to stop focusing on who you are trying to please and instead focus on who you are going to serve.

I've worked diligently to stop looking for outside validation in my life. Before taking an action, at times I *still* catch myself thinking, "What would (fill in the blank with a name, any name) think if I do that?" I catch myself pondering this question following an impulse to take action on everything, from posting on Facebook, to saying yes to an opportunity, or even expressing my own beliefs. I guess old habits really do die hard. But now when I recognize that habit, I can instead choose to validate my own actions by answering the real question that matters—*will this action serve another person? And does it align with my bigger purpose?*

Alignment, I've found, is really sexy. And I can physically feel the difference between when I'm doing something that is in alignment with my purpose versus doing it because it will please another person or avoid upsetting them. When I'm doing something that's out of alignment, it physically drains my energy. I experience angst, upset, and frustration—sometimes subtle, but always noticeable. Other times I just feel "off." The more you practice checking in with your own motivation before acting, the more you'll also start to feel the physical difference.

Now that we've touched on crappy habit #3, seeking validation outside of yourself, I'm going to turn right around and contradict myself a little bit. I am a firm believer in surrounding yourself with people who sincerely cheer you on. A tribe of like-minded individuals (even if it's just one other person) who always, without fail, see greatness in you—even when you're not showing up as your most powerful self in the moment, can inspire you to do great things. If you don't yet have someone like this in your life, don't worry. As you begin to implement these principles and step into your own power, you will start to attract people who vibe with your new energy. I didn't find a few members of my own tribe until several years into my personal development journey.

You will know you've found your tribe when you can directly ask for exactly what you need to hear from them. Sometimes having others speak greatness into your life can be a powerful way to drown out the negative self-talk on days when your inner critic's microphone is turned up to maximum volume.

My husband is one of these people in my life. I learned early on in our marriage that he does not, in fact, read minds, despite my expectation that he should (shocking, I know). So instead of getting upset, I started asking for what I needed to hear. Some days I'll ask him to tell me how much he appreciates the work I do around our house. Other days, I ask to be reminded of how he sees me as a powerhouse woman and the difference I'm making in the world. At first I felt stupid for coming right out and asking for acknowledgement. But you know what? He lights up at the opportunity to be the one who gets to fill my love cup when I need it. Now, instead of me nagging at him to clean up, I realize all that I want is to hear how much he appreciates me. Each of us loves to make a difference for others. Allowing members of your tribe to contribute to you when you most need it is often a gift to them as well. And I don't feel any less appreciated because I had to ask for it. A powerhouse woman asks for what she needs.

Just keep in mind that another person's validation can be a double-edged sword. Yes, surround yourself with those who build you up and encourage you to stretch further but don't ever allow their opinions to be a litmus test for how worthy you allow yourself to feel. I've learned that the less I look to others for validation, the more I notice that love is present—love for myself and love for others. As you build your own belief and confidence, you will become a mirror to reflect the beauty in others back to them.

Let's answer a few more questions to help you further break down any crappy habit around looking for validation outside yourself.

Who have I been looking for validation from in my life? *Examples: social media, my family, my boss, my spouse or partner.*

my parents
pretty much everyone

Who do I want to serve with my message, business, or passion project?

people who don't feel like the
best version of themselves

What are three things I can do in the next week to serve these people?

1. walk about with love & light

2. radiate positive energy

3. lead by example

Who in my life do I consider part of my tribe? Who can I ask for what I need to hear when my inner critic is unusually loud?

Matt
Sis
Mary

If I don't already have a tribe, where are a few places I could meet them? Where do positive and inspired people hang out? *Examples: personal development courses, certain networking groups, Facebook communities of people with similar interests to yours.*

Crappy Habit #4: Confusing Confidence with Having It All Together

Most people walk around in life trying to look like they have it all together. Have you noticed that? We all do such a great job of it that it can be easy to look at other people's lives and *think* that they really do have it all together—that their life really is as picture perfect as it looks on Facebook; that they never experience fear, doubt, insecurity, or anxiety, even though deep down we know that's not the case.

I don't know about you, but to me, trying to look like I have it all together is *exhausting.*

Can we just be real with each other and admit that we're all freaked the *F out*?! I am. Freaked out about whether I'll succeed, freaked out about whether I'm good enough, freaked out about whether anyone will care what I have to say, and freaked out about a whole slew of other concerns that rotate in and out of my mind daily. That's the other sneaky way that the internal critic likes to wreak havoc—by planting seeds of doubt and worry. We *all* experience our own version of it. So can we just cut the B.S. and admit that no one has it all together? We're all on the same high-to-low, up-and-down confidence roller coaster. Confidence is *not* synonymous with having it all together. Even a powerhouse woman doesn't have it all together all the time. Unfortunately, we humans tend to believe that there is a secret confidence club, and some of us aren't members. We often assume the "confident" people are all gliding through an elegant ballroom, dressed to the nines, laughing and dancing with a cocktail in their hand. Meanwhile, the rest of us peasants are standing on the bitter cold street corner, peering through the frosted glass window at this secret meeting taking place inside, wishing we could have just a few table scraps from their feast.

Okay, maybe that was a tad dramatic, but I think you get my point. There is no secret club. No one experiences consistent confidence, and no one really has it all together all the time. And whenever you're tempted to pretend otherwise (I've done it), you risk sacrificing the impact you could make. Again, this should return you to ask the question, am I trying to please people or serve them? Am I more concerned with being impressive or making an impact?

Pretending to have it all together all the time is not only completely inauthentic, it robs us of the opportunity to make an even bigger difference than we realize. I work with a group of nine- and ten-year-old girls on a weekly basis through an amazing local youth organization. We spend an hour each week coloring, creating skits, and doing activities that relate to relevant topics in their life: friendship, their sense of self, body image, and more. During our first session together, I asked the girls what they hoped to get out of the program. Their most popular answer? More confidence. These sweet little souls are already seeking a feeling that many adults spend their entire lives pursuing. Then it hit me—we all have a tremendous duty to show the next generation that genuine confidence comes from within, that it's always available, that this beautiful life is full of ups and downs, that experiencing doubts and insecurities makes us human, that it's okay not to have it all together all the time, and that there is incredible beauty in vulnerability.

Let me tell you something else. I have a major sweet tooth. I've been known to say that I have a special compartment in my stomach reserved just for sweets. No matter how full I am, I can always unlock this secret little compartment and make room for dessert after a meal. It's a gift, I know. If it was my last meal on earth, and I had to choose which dessert I was going to savor, without question, it would be every last bite of a flourless chocolate molten lava cake. You know, the kind that when you cut into it, a river of glorious rich chocolate goodness comes pouring out. That's my favorite part, the warm gooey stuff. It's the whole essence of the cake. I think humans are a lot like that, too. Our gooey stuff underneath the outer shell—the soft, vulnerable, sometimes runny emotions—is the most beautiful part of us. Just like courage isn't the absence of fear, confidence isn't the absence of vulnerability. Having confidence often means being willing to fail and let others see our failure. If you're willing to break through your outer shell and expose your gooey parts, you'll come to know that your deepest failures may offer another human being a tremendous gift.

Don't get me wrong. There are times when it is absolutely appropriate to stand tall and "fake it till you make it." Then there are other times when your power lies in being able to admit that you're a human being with real insecurities and that you bring those insecurities along with you as you move forward. The true beauty of vulnerability is found in being able to say, "Yes, I'm freaked out about reaching the crazy audacious goals I have, and that's ok. If I can move forward in spite of my fear, so can you."

Press pause for a few minutes to look at where crabby habit #4, confusing confidence with having it all together, may be getting in the way of your inner confidence shining through:

Describe a scenario where you felt you had to pretend you have it all together.

How could you show a little vulnerability in this area and help others who may feel the same way?

WHEN IN DOUBT, CHOOSE LOVE

As I hope you've already seen, I'm not writing any of this content as someone who has confidence (or life) all figured out. I'm constantly learning how to tap into my own inner confidence. The fastest way to reconnect with my most authentic, confident self is by taking a close look at where I may have slipped back into one of these four crappy habits. I usually find that I'm blocking my own feelings of confidence with a combination of inaction, negative self-talk, looking for validation in the wrong places, or holding on to an unrealistic expectation of having it all together.

It's also important to realize that everyone around you is on their own version of the same journey. After reading this book, now you'll have some tools that they may not yet have. I like to remind myself that I never know what internal battles someone else is fighting. The best gift I can give another human being is pure, unconditional love, but neither you nor I can give someone else love from a well that is empty. So before you give love to another, give love to yourself. Love is the fastest way to access your ever-present confidence.

My biggest takeaway from this chapter :

LET'S RECAP

- Broken confidence can be one of the biggest roadblocks in bringing your nudge to life.
- We always have access to confidence, although it may not always feel that way.
- The roller coaster of high-to-low, up-and-down self-confidence is a normal experience when you're pursuing a goal bigger than yourself. That's exactly how growth is supposed to feel, so hang in there, Sister!
- Your access to the ever-present confidence within you is to look closely at your underlying beliefs and habits.
- The only way to build confidence around a new skill is by taking action (and the right kind of action).
- Your inner critic is not your friend. Her negative running commentary is not the truth.
- Surround yourself with people who can build you up when you need it, but don't allow the opinions of others dictate how worthy you feel.
- No one has it all together all the time. Your authenticity and vulnerability may be your greatest access to making a difference with people.

POWERHOUSE ACTION PLAN:
HOW TO BREAK CRAPPY CONFIDENCE HABITS FOR GOOD

We've illuminated some truths behind the four habits that most often rob us of confidence: inaction, what you say to yourself about yourself, looking for validation from outside sources, and confusing confidence with having it all together. Your challenge this week is to bring awareness to where these habits show up in your daily life. Awareness, without judgment, is the first step in reframing old crappy habits into those that enhance your confidence. Remember, these four harmful habits have probably been running you amuck for years, so don't expect to eliminate them overnight.

In the second half of this book, we'll do a lot of work around creating new beliefs and habits. For now, let's arm you with antidotes to use whenever you notice a crappy belief or habit running the show. I'll give you some examples of what I do to course correct when I feel disconnected from my confidence power source, but feel free to come up with your own.

Habit: Inaction. Resisting the action you *know* you need to take to move forward.

Antidote: Ask, what can I accomplish next to move forward toward my goals? Focus on a small next step (only one thing) until it's accomplished.

Examples: Write or create content, make a phone call, have a difficult conversation with someone.

Habit: Negative self-talk. Feeling less than rock-star confident.

Antidote: Check in with what your self-talk sounds like. What have you been saying to yourself? Remind yourself that your inner critic is reading from a script you wrote, which means you can change the script by reframing negative self-talk into something new.

Example: I'm not enough. **Reframe***: I'm doing my best. I am a beautiful work in progress.*

Habit: Looking for validation from outside sources.

Antidote: Ask, who am I trying to impress? Then ask, who am I out to serve and what will add value to their lives?

Example: I'm trying to impress my peers. **Reframe***: I am out to serve women, so they can feel genuine confidence at any moment they choose.*

Habit: Feeling like you need to have it all together.

Antidote: Take the focus off yourself. Do something to contribute to another person.

Example: Call someone and share how much you appreciate them. Buy a stranger's coffee.

Throughout the week, use the space below to journal about what you're noticing. Which of the four habits do you currently wrestle with most frequently (inaction, negative self-talk, looking for outside validation, feeling like you have to have it all together)?

Which beliefs or habits do you find the hardest to break or reframe?

When we started talking about the unproductive habits threatening to take you off track from your nudge, I told you that the three C's—confidence, comparison, and comfort zone—are all interconnected. There isn't anything that puts cracks in healthy confidence faster than comparison. Let's look at that one next, shall we?

POWER #3:
CHOOSE COLLABORATION OVER COMPARISON

You are a creative and inspired human being. As a powerhouse woman, it's who you are by design. But if you're looking for the fastest way to kill off your natural creativity and inspiration (not to mention your self-confidence), start comparing yourself to others. I would know. I'm an expert in self-sabotage, and my weapon of choice is comparison. If there is one crappy habit that needs to go more than any other, it's this one.

The word "comparison" is almost too soft because what's really behind comparing yourself to other people is some pretty ugly stuff—judgment, criticism, and envy to name a few. It wasn't until I started to tell the truth about the role I allowed comparison and criticism to play in my life that I was able to create space for something new. Even if you don't think you struggle with comparison, I encourage you to look closely with a commitment to discover something new. There may be a hidden breakthrough standing between you, and the business or passion project you want to create.

Have you ever noticed that it's impossible to think of new creative ideas while simultaneously comparing yourself to someone else? Comparison shrinks you. It's total self-sabotage, a cleverly disguised excuse to stay where you are and not move forward in pursuit of what you're being called to do. *That person is already doing what I wanted to do, sharing the message I wanted to share, and doing it better. . . . so why bother? I will never get to where she is in her business. What's wrong with me that I don't have those results? Wow, she sure is lucky! If only I had her money/connections/good looks, then I would be successful, too.* Do any of these thoughts sound familiar? You may not say them out loud. I don't. But as much as I hate to admit it, I've certainly caught myself having these thoughts on more than one occasion.

Where do we learn to compare anyhow? For starters, from a young age we're constantly fed images by the media that send a clear message—*You, young lady, are not beautiful/smart/cool/pretty/ skinny/popular or good enough unless you buy THIS product.* We are trained to look for flaws. We're shown countless images designed to make us realize that we don't measure up. If even a professional model doesn't live up to the perfectly airbrushed and Photoshopped version of herself, what hope is there for us five-foot-something non-airbrushed beauties? The entire advertising industry is built to prey upon our insecurities and position "solutions" to fix them. The only problem is, you can't buy self-love. It doesn't come in a bottle.

Whether the media, a family member, or other social influences taught you to compare yourself to others, blaming the source doesn't solve anything. Breaking up with the toxic comparison habit starts with taking back 100 percent responsibility, not for the actions of others, but for your own reactions and the negative effects your reactions have on your own life and on other people's lives, too. You may not be able to change the influences that taught you to compare, but you can control your response to it, which is where all your power lies. Here's how to begin rewiring the effect comparison has on you and take back your power.

NOT ENOUGH

I can't say with certainty exactly where I learned to compare. I don't know whether it was from the media or from other influences. But my earliest memory of this ugly habit dates all the way back to elementary school. I can remember the sunny spring day it first happened on the playground with my friends. At eight years old, I am far more concerned with mastering the double Dutch jump rope than with what boys think of me. As I head over to the large blacktop area under the flagpole where an intense double Dutch session is about to go down, I pass a group of boys from my class and overhear them talking about the girls, ranking us based on who they like best and who they think is the prettiest.

It's all very innocent. They aren't saying any of it to my face and probably have no idea I can hear the conversation. The intent isn't malicious in any way; however, in that moment, I become acutely aware that there is something *different* about me, and not in a good way. I start to notice things that I hadn't noticed before. *The prettiest girls aren't wearing thick glasses like mine. The boys like Meghan the best. She's tall.*

For the record, they ranked me third overall. In a small private school class with only five girls total, I didn't consider this a personal victory. And I didn't leave the impact of this event on the playground that day. Although I didn't make the connection until my late twenties, during that innocent playground conversation, I decided, subconsciously, that I was always going to be compared to other people (particularly women), and there would always be someone better than me. I might as well have tattooed a number three on my forehead because in that moment, I unknowingly sentenced myself to a life of never feeling good enough.

Over the next 20 years, my playground decision about comparisons, especially among woman, played out in a variety of ways. I wanted badly to join the high school dance team, but I was so intimidated by the more seasoned dancers that I left the first day of tryouts in tears, never to return. I also avoided social situations where I'd be in groups of women I didn't know. When I walked into a room, I could instantly pick out the woman who I thought was the prettiest, or who was wearing the best outfit, or who had the most poise and confidence. And it didn't even have to be a physical attribute; I could find any aspect of another woman to unfavorably compare myself to. The internal conversations happened subconsciously, and the message was loud and clear: *I am not enough.*

My use of comparison impacted every single relationship in my life. It determined whether I would go after opportunities or not and whether I would step out of my comfort zone or not. Little by little, I allowed the walls of comparison to start closing in on my life, making me smaller, shrinking down my dreams and goals to fit into the confines of comparison's walls—until I realized I had a say in the matter.

NORMALIZING COMPARISON

It took a weekend personal development intensive for me to wake up and confront the role I had allowed comparison to play in my life. And thank God I received that wake-up call when I did. You see, most of my comparison was going on in the background, subconsciously, up until then. It worked much like an app running in the background on your cell phone—even when you're not actively using the app, it's draining your phone's battery. Comparison had been draining my emotional battery for twenty years. Maybe you can relate. But here's the craziest part of it all. As I started to share my experience with people, and my realization that comparison had been running my life ever since that fateful day on the playground, the most common rationale I heard about comparisons was, "Well, isn't that *normal?*" Maybe you've found yourself thinking the same thing. At one point in my life, I might have even said the same: comparison is unavoidable, can't be controlled, and therefore, it's out of our hands—out of our control. But let's stop to ask ourselves, *is it really?*

When did we collectively decide that we are okay with comparison being "normal"?

That we have no say in the matter of stopping it, that we can't do anything about it? Was there a secret meeting that I missed? I'm sorry, but I'm not buying it. And we're not doing ourselves any favors by accepting the damaging effects of comparison as "normal" in our lives. True, you may not be able to stop every initial comparison thought that enters your consciousness, but you can choose to accept or reject those thoughts. By refusing to normalize comparison, you control the effect that comparing yourself to others has on your life. And if you're willing to reconsider how "normal" you will allow comparison to be, I'll teach you how I've been able to reframe these thoughts to work for me, not against me.

PATTERN INTERRUPT

As much as I'd love to tell you that I've eliminated comparison from my life, you already know it's not quite that simple. What I *have* done is found ways to reframe these thoughts and their effects on me. Most of my comparison thoughts and the self-criticism they bring happen subconsciously. I can be scrolling social media and all of a sudden, seemingly out of nowhere, I feel an icky, unwelcome energy wash over me like I'm slowly being covered in Nickelodeon goo. My shoulders slump forward, my energy drains, and I start to notice a downward spiral of negative self-talk. I'm not even *conscious* of what caused the icky energy. All I know is that one moment I'm scrolling past adorable baby photos and hilarious cat videos, and the next moment I'm acutely aware of how not-awesome I am.

This cycle of social media self-sabotage went on for years until one day when I noticed the familiar icky energy show up, and I actually stopped to ask, *"Okay. Whoooaaaa! Where the hell is this coming from?"* I wanted to identify the source of the ick, so I could send it packing. When I slowed down and replayed the thoughts and events leading up to the icky energy feeling, I was able to see so clearly that I had simply scrolled past something on social media that triggered a comparison—someone's business success, a great set of abs, a photo of a friend on a beautiful beach with an umbrella drink in her hand—and without even realizing it, my little subconscious voice whispered *you don't have THAT.*

Have you ever experienced something similar? If so, telling the truth about it is the first step to freeing up your energy and refocusing it on the awesome business and life you're creating. Start to notice what your subconscious voice says when you're deep into comparison mode. *I don't deserve that. I'm not good enough. I'm not worthy of love/happiness/success. I'll never reach my goal.* The ugliest versions of my comparison thoughts often include a judgment about the other person too, not just me. *Why did she get that opportunity? What's so great about her? She doesn't deserve it. I hate her. It's not fair.* Whatever it is, put that B.S. on loudspeaker and tell the truth about how much you've let comparisons run the show up until this point. If you don't, the icky energy and negative self-talk that results can persist for an hour, a day, or can even take you off track from your dreams completely.

It took me a little while to get to the heart of the subconscious underlying message of my comparison thoughts, but doing so is a powerful step toward interrupting the pattern. Start by identifying the moment when you notice a shift in your energy. One moment you're feeling great; the next moment you're hyper-aware of your perceived flaws. Stop to replay whatever happened leading up to that feeling. Were you scrolling social media, listening to someone share a success, looking through a magazine, or lost in a random train of thought? See if you can pinpoint the trigger. Where did comparison rear its ugly head?

Once you identify the most likely suspect that triggered a comparison, stop to ask yourself, *what did I say in that moment*? It's typically some version of "not enough." *I'm not good enough, smart enough, successful enough, pretty enough.* Pick your poison. This part takes some work and a willingness to be 100 percent honest, even with the ugly judgments focused on other people.

When you're honest about it, you can start to separate these thoughts as not really you, at least not your highest, powerhouse self. These thoughts are just your inner critic, broadcasting on a different radio station. When your inner critic goes unchecked, this victim mentality subconsciously plays on repeat in the background, leading you to dislike yourself and other people, and leaving you to wonder why you're not moving forward toward your goals.

Awareness is the first step in breaking up with the comparison habit. The second step is choosing a new thought to replace the critical one. Interrupt the pattern entirely by consciously choosing something new—something that empowers you *and* whoever you're comparing yourself to. Even if this is all happening internally and never shared out loud, it's useless to replace negative energy with more negative energy by turning a comparison thought around in a way that degrades another person. You know, something to the effect of *she's not really that beautiful. Look at that huge nose!* We rise by lifting others up, not by tearing them down. The fastest way I'm able to turn around my deep dark critical thoughts is to reframe them from I don't have that to an empowering mantra or expression of gratitude. Let me share a few examples that might help you start to reframe your comparison thoughts as you notice them.

COMPARING YOURSELF TO THE HIGHLIGHT REEL

Do you ever notice that you're usually comparing your worst to someone else's best? We criticize our own lives based on how they stack up to another person's highlight reel, or we judge the beginning of our journey against the middle of someone else's. Many of us work so hard to prove to ourselves that we aren't capable, beautiful, successful, or good enough, that we'll find someone with totally different life circumstances and hold up the mirror of comparison. Here are a few suggestions for how to start interrupting this pattern:

Her body is perfect.

New mantra: "Clearly she has put in the work to have the body she has, and I appreciate the inspiration!" or "I'm a beautiful work in progress," or "I'm grateful to have a body that is physically capable of exercise."

I wish I had her life.

New mantra: "Three things I'm most grateful for in my life right now are . . ."

She doesn't have five kids like I do, but why can't I have her energy?

New mantra: "I get to choose how I feel, and today I choose happiness and vibrant energy."

Sometimes I'll even stop and say a little prayer, thanking God (or insert whoever you pray to) for blessing that person with the gift that they have, one that I may have, a moment earlier, caught myself comparing myself to. Whatever interrupts the pattern and refocuses my mind on something empowering will work. Besides, you can truly only compare yourself to the woman you were yesterday. There will always be evidence for your shortcomings if you look for it, and doing so won't get you any closer to your goals.

COMPETITION MASQUERADING AS COMPARISON

The real danger behind comparison and self-criticism is that it threatens our capacity for growth by creating a "me versus them" world instead of "all of us together." Comparing yourself with another person is a form of competition. When we compare, we create a viewpoint that other women (or people for that matter) are our competition, and with that perspective, we risk missing out on what we could *learn* from them. Maybe, for example, your comparison thoughts are creating "competition" with the person who would have taught you the lesson you needed to learn, passed on a key piece of wisdom, or introduced you to your next big client—or even the love of your life. Powerhouse women collaborate, not compete, with each other. Comparison and competition are the enemy—not whoever it is we think we're competing against. When I notice this version of comparison come up, I typically reframe it to a mantra of "and so am I."

I'll never have her confidence.

New mantra: "She is a powerhouse, *and so am I.*"

Why is she so successful, and I'm not?

New mantra: "I'm grateful to have amazing role models to look up to in business," or "I may not be at that point in my business yet, but I will be. Rock on girlfriend. You inspire me."

Don't worry if the replacement thought sounds like a complete lie at first. Over time, you'll start to believe the new ideas you're planting. Keep feeding your mind new thoughts of gratitude, and it will start to seek out more to be grateful for.

YOUR INNER GPS

You can *always* find someone better, stronger, faster, prettier, or smarter if you're looking for it. Much like a GPS tells you how to reach the destination you have programmed it for, your mind will naturally find whatever you tell it to focus on. If you program your mind to focus on finding evidence for your deepest fears and insecurities, you better believe it will find evidence.

Ever notice how when you get a new car, you start noticing that same make and model everywhere? Or when you download a new ringtone for your phone, it's as though everyone around you went out and downloaded that exact same ringtone too because it's all you hear? The cars and the ringtones were there all along. You've just tuned your awareness to pick up on them. The mind does the same thing with your fears and insecurities.

What you focus on, you'll always find.

Much like the GPS on your phone needs to be programmed with a destination or it's utterly useless; your mind is the same way. If you don't feed it something positive to focus on, instead of taking you toward your goal, it will often default to old patterns (like comparison). When I notice myself comparing more than usual, I take an honest inventory and look at whether or not I'm focused on a goal and purpose bigger than myself. When I'm not, I notice that I'm always more critical of what others around me are doing. But when I'm focused on who I can contribute to, or the next big nudge that is trying to get my attention, there is very little time or energy to be playing the comparison game. By the way, don't beat yourself up if you notice comparison and criticism happening even more now that you've tuned your awareness to it. Each comparison is an opportunity to choose a new thought and reprogram your subconscious mind to pick up on evidence that you're a total rock star (because you are).

My biggest takeaway from this chapter:

LET'S RECAP

- Comparison is the fastest way to kill off your natural creativity and inspiration.
- You don't have to accept comparison as "normal." You can choose to reframe comparison thoughts and take back your power.
- Reframe comparison by noticing it, replaying the underlying subconscious message, and consciously turning it into an empowering mantra or expression of gratitude.

POWERHOUSE ACTION PLAN:
COLLABORATION TRUMPS COMPARISON

For this lesson, your challenge is to notice when you slip into comparison mode and consciously choose a new mantra or expression of gratitude. Treat it like a game. See how fast you can flip from a draining comparison thought to an empowering thought. Use the space below to journal about what you're noticing as you tune your awareness to comparison habits over the next several days.

Are there particular environments or scenarios that trigger comparison for you? *Examples: social media, the gym, when I set a big goal or take an action outside my comfort zone, etc.*

What do you say about yourself in these moments of comparison? If you were to put it on loudspeaker, what's the underlying message? *Examples: I'm not good enough. I'm stupid. I'm not worthy of love/success.*

Write out a few examples of the most persistent comparison thoughts you notice. Then write out the mantra or gratitude that you are going to use to reframe those thoughts in the future.

Example: Persistent comparison: I wish I had her life.

New mantra: Three things I'm most grateful for in my life right now are...

Who would you like to collaborate with, but you find you often compare yourself to?

POWER #4:
DITCH COMFORT FOR GROWTH

The third musketeer in the trio of habits due for a breakup is comfort. The phrase "get out of your comfort zone" gets thrown around a lot in personal development, but have you ever stopped to think about what "comfort zone" really means and how it relates to your goals? No matter which dictionary you consult, the consensus seems to be that your "comfort zone" is a mental state where you experience low stress and a sense of control. I imagine lounging in a plush robe while being served chocolate-covered strawberries and indulging in round-the-clock foot massages. Relaxed. Unplugged. Without a care in the world. If you ask me, that sounds like a fantastic place to hang out. So why is the personal development world obsessed with encouraging us to step out of our comfy, cozy, low-stress environment?

For one reason and one reason only—because *growth* doesn't happen within the confines of your comfort zone. Buzz kill. I know.

And growth, as it turns out, is usually vital to you bringing your nudge to life. Growth is necessary if you are going to start your business, write your book, or create the passion project you've been thinking about for years. If everything you needed to achieve your goal was already within your current comfort zone—the thoughts, skills, and habits needed to produce the outcome you want—then it's pretty safe to say you would already have the outcome or at least be able to go out and make it happen quickly.

Typically, there's a gap between where you are now and where you're going next. The bridge to the other side is called growth. The only problem is, standing on the edge of the gap between your bigger purpose and your current reality will often feel like standing on the edge of a steep cliff, looking down at the sharp rocks and rushing waters three hundred feet below you. It's no wonder that instead of leaping into the unknown, hoping you don't fall to your death, your natural human tendency is to retreat to safety and assume the fetal position.

The world is full of people who are perfectly happy inside the confines of their comfort zones, but not you, powerhouse. You're a dreamer. There's no comfort zone big enough to hold the purpose that you are designed for.

And, for that reason, you must leap.

Now, I'll be the first to admit that taking the leap into the unknown is much easier said than done. To support myself when contemplating taking my own great leaps of faith, I've saved all the inspirational quotes I could find and reposted them on social media. You know, the ones with flowery sentiments like, *"A comfort zone is a beautiful place, but nothing ever grows there."* I've listened to countless podcasts, read hundreds of books on success, personal growth, and achievement, and I've invested thousands of dollars attending personal development seminars. Yet no matter how many times I've heard someone say that growth happens outside of where I'm comfortable, my natural tendency is to resist it. I *loathe* being new at things. Thinking back to new experiences makes me cringe no matter how long ago they happened—starting at a new school, learning a new job, or meeting a brand new group of people. And don't even get me started on my first few (and totally awkward) dates. Being new at things is so freaking uncomfortable.

For years, my desire to stay comfortable and in control ran the show more than I would like to admit. I took only the college classes I knew I could ace, stayed in a toxic relationship far past its expiration date, avoided social situations where I would have to meet new people, and stayed in my corporate job for months after I knew I was ready to make the leap into my own business.

But I was also a master of disguise. From the outside, it certainly looked like I was a fearless high achiever. I could operate at 70 percent and fool people into thinking it was my 100 percent. I wasn't fooling myself, though. Deep down I knew the truth: I had a lot more to give. I wasn't stretching myself. I wasn't growing. I was willing to get uncomfortable but only to the degree that I was comfortable with. Being unwilling to step out and take a risk—of failing, looking and feeling awkward, or experiencing disappointment—is probably the number one thing that has slowed down the progress I've made and the goals I've achieved so far. Sometimes I wonder, though, how many other opportunities I missed along the way by not being willing to try.

When I started to learn about how the brain works and where the feeling of "comfort" comes from, I was finally able to loosen the death grip on my own comfort zone and realize that I'm not a total crazy person. It's always a good day when you find out you're not a crazy person.

THIS IS YOUR BRAIN ON COMFORT

I'm kind of a nerd when it comes to learning about how the brain works, especially if it's going to help me understand how to perform better in my business and life. One of the first books I read when I started my business was *The Answer*, co-written by John Assaraf and Murray Smith. This book helped me to radically shift my view of "comfort" and understand the grip it had on my business and life. John Assaraf is a serial entrepreneur and CEO of a brain-research company called NeuroGym. He's been researching the brain for the past twenty years to help people achieve their life's purpose. In *The Answer*, John talks about a powerful regulating mechanism that controls your brain's response to change, much like a thermostat regulates the temperature of a room.

Think about the role of a thermostat. It will always work to bring the temperature of a room up or down to the exact degree it has been programmed for. Even if a momentary change in temperature occurs—like if you open the front door during a blizzard, allowing a gust of cold air inside—the thermostat will kick in and bring the temperature of the room back up to the original set point. Your brain has a similar internal regulating mechanism. You could even say that the brain's "set point" is your comfort zone. Any time you deviate outside of this zone, it triggers your internal "thermostat." The scientific name for this internal regulator is the *psycho cybernetic mechanism*, a term coined by Dr. Maxwell Malz in the 1950s. We'll just call it "the psycho" for short, a fitting name for its often delusional behavior.

Deep down, the brain has absolutely no interest in you growing or changing. Its main goal is to keep you safe from actual danger. The internal regulating mechanisms that freak out when you deviate from your comfort zone are the same mechanisms controlling your heartbeat and breathing, two functions that are pretty important to your survival. Any change to your breathing or heartbeat could actually result in death, so the psycho draws the conclusion that ALL change equals death. Any time you go to make a change that will take you out of your comfort zone, the psycho will tell your brain to release a chemical warning signal in an attempt to sabotage the mission and keep you "safe." Your nervous system will often interpret this signal as doubt, fear, or stress, which causes your mind to respond in the same way your body would if you jumped into an ice bath. Everything in you wants *out* of the situation—and quick.

This automatic brain response was super helpful in the era when being chased by a wooly mammoth was a very real possibility. The brain was always on high alert. The same fight-or- flight tendency is present today, but the brain can't distinguish between growth and change in a positive direction and *actual* danger. The problem isn't that the psycho sends an alert signal; the real problem is our *interpretation* of the signal. When your nervous system picks up on the feelings of doubt, fear, or anxiety, you react the same as if you were facing a real threat—fight, flight, or freeze. In reality, these invisible sirens are just a warning sign for you to stop, check in, and make sure that what you're about to do isn't actually endangering your life. You're usually not in actual danger; you're just growing.

How does this relate to you, your life, and your business or passion project? Well, *any* attempt to grow and change will eventually trip the alarm of the psycho cybernetic system. This includes any change to your finances, your physical body, and your relationships. Even a positive change in the direction you want to go will cause the psycho to have a mini-meltdown. Embrace these little warning signals from the psycho; they typically mean that you are dangerously close to your next breakthrough. The psycho is just warning you that something is about to change.

I can't stress how vital it is to consciously work toward breaking up with your "comfortable" habits. Your brain *needs* change in order to grow and adapt. Deviating from what is comfortable and familiar forces the brain to make new neural connections. These new connections translate into the new habits that will move you forward. But to create lasting change, you must recalibrate the thermostat to support where you want to go. Everything we'll talk about throughout the rest of this book is aimed at doing exactly that—changing deeply rooted beliefs and habits into those that support your vision, so they no longer occur as a "threat." You will learn to reprogram your "psycho" using your imagination and to reinforce your vision with language and action so the new habits will stick.

Don't think that you have to get this whole comfort zone thing handled before you can take action. You can jump into action *now* and learn the rest along the way. For starters, I'll teach you an easy technique that I use to bypass the psycho whenever I feel a nudge into action.

FIVE SECONDS

If the brain is wired to resist growth and change, but growth is a necessary factor in you bringing your nudge to life, what can you do to bypass the brain's operating system and install some new software? All it takes is five seconds, more specifically, a simple and effective technique called "the five second rule," coined by Mel Robbins, a best-selling author, speaker, and CNN contributor, in her brilliant TEDx talk, "How to Stop Screwing Yourself Over."

As Mel explains, your brain has two speeds—autopilot and emergency brake. And guess which one your brain likes better? Yep, autopilot. Now that we've dug into the science behind comfort, it's easier to understand why your brain loves to coast on autopilot. Autopilot requires no change, no perceived threat. So, naturally, any time you go to deviate outside of your normal routine (autopilot), your brain pulls an invisible emergency brake to stop you. Have you ever experienced that? You think of a person you want to call, but making that call is a little intimidating. Your mind says, *You know what? That person is probably busy right now. Tomorrow would be a better time to call.* Emergency brake. Or you see a cute guy across the room and think I should go talk to him, but when you go to move, your feet are cemented in place by an invisible force. The brain comes up with a perfectly valid excuse for not moving, something like, *He's almost too good looking, so there's no way he's actually a decent guy. He'll probably break my heart.* To have any chance of growing and changing or deviating from autopilot, you must act before the emergency brake is triggered.

I don't know about you, but I rarely *feel* like doing what's required in order to grow. In fact, it usually scares the hell out of me. For this reason, Mel explains that any break from your normal routine is going to require force. And you have exactly five seconds to act on an impulse before your brain hijacks the mission and pulls the emergency brake. It's as simple as this—the moment you have an impulse to take an action that will move you closer to your goals, count down in your mind *five . . . four . . . three . . . two . . . one.* And by the time you reach one, you must physically move to act on the impulse. Start walking toward the cute guy. Pick up the phone and dial the person's number. Throw on your tennis shoes, step out of your front door, and go for a walk. Whatever it is, take the first small action on your impulse before you get to *one.*

What's so special about five seconds? Well, for starters, giving your mind a countdown creates the perfect distraction from the thoughts about why you *shouldn't* take the action you're thinking about. You know, the peanut gallery in your own mind with all kinds of opinions about whether or not you feel like doing it, whether it's the "right" time to take that action, or what might happen as a result—all the thoughts and excuses your mind comes up with to avoid taking action and getting uncomfortable. Counting down is just enough to interrupt your mind's normal pattern of sabotage, creating a momentary distraction that allows you to make that first move before your mind realizes what is happening.

Are there some situations and decisions in life that require more thoughtful consideration? Absolutely. I'm not suggesting that you make impulsive decisions that could harm you physically or financially. The five-second rule is helpful when creating new habits around the actions you know deep down will move you forward toward your goals, and that you may be uncomfortable taking. These could be actions like making a phone call to a prospective client, walking into a networking event where you won't know anyone, or posting your first Facebook Live video.

I decided to put this theory to the test in my own life, starting with an example Mel Robbins shares about getting out of bed in the morning. I admit, I've become quite fond of my snooze button. We're besties. Hitting snooze four or five times each morning is not uncommon in my life. Typically, since I am my own boss and work from home, I don't have to wake up at a certain time. I take full advantage of this particular perk. Getting out of bed before 7:00 a.m. seems like the kind of punishment you'd use to convince criminals of war to share state secrets. So an early wake-up call made the perfect test for the five-second rule. Nothing in me wanted to do it. The game was simple. I set my alarm for an hour earlier than normal. When the alarm went off, I had exactly five seconds to throw off the covers and stand up out of bed. No delay. No snooze button.

The night before Day One of my five-second-rule test, I set an alarm for 6:00 a.m. I even changed my alarm ringtone to a jazzy little upbeat tune, anything to shock my brain into playing along with my little experiment. Before going to sleep, I visualized my perfect morning. I saw myself waking up easily, standing up out of bed, and giving a little stretch with a glowing smile ready to face the day. There may have even been some angels singing too. I imagine the morning going exactly according to plan. Then I go to sleep.

At 6:00 a.m., the alarm went off. The new ringtone proved to be a welcome distraction to my brain. I began the countdown: five . . . four . . . three . . . two. I noticed the counting does interrupt the normal train of thought that typically welcomes me into a new day: *You don't have any important calls or meetings scheduled this morning. Ten more minutes won't hurt anything. You worked so hard yesterday; you've earned this extra beauty sleep. You know, I heard that getting twelve hours of sleep each night is clinically proven to prevent wrinkles after thirty. . .* My peanut gallery was suspiciously quiet this morning. Maybe they hit snooze and slept in this time?

My feet had to hit the floor by one, so naturally I waited until the very last millisecond. I also counted in super slo-mo. My arm flopped dramatically on the bed as I threw the covers off. It wasn't pretty. I immediately regretted the decision, but I kept my word and stood up out of bed. That's the worst part anyway, right? Leaving the snuggly warm cocoon of your bed, along with the loving embrace of your partner or pet? The first few seconds *really* sucked. But as I stumbled to the bathroom to put in my contacts, a tiny cheerleader in my brain chanted, *You did it! You can do anything! You're amazing!* Thanks, tiny cheerleader. Right back at you.

By the time I finished my morning cup of coffee, I transformed into a fully functioning human being, like Cinderella after her fairy godmother waves the magic wand. Maybe I *could* get used to this 6:00 a.m. business.

The first few days of my new wake-up ritual were the hardest. After a week of faithfully practicing the five-second rule each morning, something amazing happened. I started to wake up *before* the alarm even went off—not just wake up, go back to sleep, and wait for the alarm. No, I was getting up and starting my day before 6:00 a.m. Who even does that anyway? I feel like I should get some kind of trophy for this accomplishment or at least a Girl Scout badge. I guess it's true what my inspirational quotes on Pinterest say: as you grow, your comfort zone grows along with you. Who knew?

Waking up early without hitting snooze, though, is a metaphor for a much bigger issue. As Mel Robbins points out, we aren't just pressing snooze on our alarm clocks each morning, we are hitting the snooze button *on our lives*, on our ideas, and on our nudges. We say and think things like *I'll work on that idea later. I'm too busy. I've got too much on my plate to think about that business I want to start. I'll make that call tomorrow.* Our problem isn't the quantity or quality of genius ideas, it's that we're hitting the snooze button when the ideas nudge us. And by doing so, we delay the difference we could be making for the people we want to impact. The cure for a snooze-button life? When you experience a spark of inspiration or an impulse to take action on a nudge—act on it. Within five seconds. And watch that beautiful comfort zone start to expand and grow as you do. Even the smallest action step in the right direction will interrupt your snooze button life and move you forward. Every awkward step, every nervous phone call, and every brave action will compound to bring your nudge to life.

GROW BABY GROW

Let's be real with each other: *nothing* is more uncomfortable than doing nothing about your dreams or ignoring the nudge that you are meant for more. In doing so, you are ignoring your soul. Growth and change are always uncomfortable at first, especially if you're reaching for really big goals and doing things you've never done before. You have a choice every day between the temporary pain of taking a scary step in the direction of your dream or the dull nagging discomfort of an unfulfilled nudge.

In the next few chapters, we'll talk about how to train your mind to work for, not against you. I'll also share how language plays a big role in bringing your nudge to life. For now, just start to observe your comfort zone at play and what opportunities and actions it tricks you into seeing as a "threat" to your survival. Spoiler alert—those are typically the exact actions you need to take to get where you want to go.

My biggest takeaway from this chapter:

LET'S RECAP

- Growth happens outside the confines of your comfort zone.
- Growth is necessary to bring your nudge to life.
- Your brain is wired to see all change as a legitimate threat to your survival, which is why stepping outside your comfort zone is often accompanied by feelings of fear and stress.
- Feelings of fear and stress are just a warning sign to stop, check in, and make sure that what you're about to do isn't actually endangering your life.
- Your brain needs change in order to grow and adapt. Deviating from what is comfortable and familiar forces the brain to make new neural connections, and these new connections translate into the new habits that will move you forward.
- The five-second rule is a helpful tool for bypassing your brain's automatic response to stop you from changing and growing.

POWERHOUSE ACTION PLAN:
RELEASE THE DEATH GRIP ON YOUR
COMFORT ZONE

In what area(s) of your life have you been operating within your comfort zone?

This week, your challenge is to find one opportunity each day to put the five-second rule to the test. When you have an impulse to take action, act within the first five seconds. Use the space below to journal about what you learned from doing this.

Examples: Act when you have the impulse to make a phone call, when you see someone across the room at a networking event that you want to talk to, or when you leave work exhausted, but promised yourself you'd hit the gym before driving home.

A FRESH START

We've identified some of the biggest unproductive habits that may be getting in the way of you making the impact you want to make. But don't necessarily expect your relationship with the three C's to end overnight. Any current habits around confidence, comparison, and your comfort zone took you years to develop. It may take weeks, months, or even years for you to consciously reprogram them. As you do, your level of success, fulfillment, and happiness will dramatically increase. Now that you've made the conscious decision to break up with the three C's (regardless of how long it takes), let's get to the good stuff.

You're a woman on the prowl. Except instead of looking for a lover, you're searching for something far more important. You're in the market for the beliefs and habits that will *love you* back—those that will carry you, your message, and your impact forward. I'm going to share what I've found to be the most fundamental and effective strategies to get out of your own way and let your light shine. And it all starts with the three most powerful forces you have at your disposal—your mind, your words, and your actions.

PART 3: YOUR MIND

When you break up with old habits and clear space in your mind for something new, it allows you to view the world through a different filter, or mindset. With a new mindset, you can see things differently. New opportunities start to appear. Opportunities that may have been there all along, but you couldn't see them before.

Think of your mindset as the operating system behind everything you think, say, and do. As you go through life, your experiences are carefully documented and filed away in this operating system. Your mind then uses these stored files to evaluate the world around you and pick out the most important information amid billions of stimuli present in every moment. This filtering capability is a *good* thing—unless of course your mind is filtering out ideas, people, or opportunities that would take you to the next level. Most of this filtering happens at a subconscious level. It's a *habit*. And like any habit, the way your mind filters the world around you can be changed. A simple shift could result in a massive difference in your results.

I've always been fascinated by what makes certain people successful, specifically the beliefs and habits that drive them. As I've studied successful people and observed how they operate, I started to notice four common themes when it comes to their mindset: (1) they focus on what they want (not on what they don't want), (2) they view resistance as necessary and productive, (3) they operate from a sincere place of gratitude, and (4) they approach life with an abundant mentality. We'll dive deeper into each of these themes in the next four chapters, and fine-tune the operating system of your mind to support your success.

POWER #5:
ADJUST YOUR FOCUS

I've never considered myself a racing enthusiast, but I recently listened to a fascinating interview with an Indy car driver that totally changed my perspective. Did you know that success in professional racing and success in life have a lot in common? I didn't.

During the interview, the pro car driver talked about two keys to success in his sport. First, you need to be hyper focused, yet have your body remain completely relaxed—not an easy feat when you're speeding around a track at two hundred miles per hour. His second key to success? If you're losing control of the car, do not, under any circumstances, look at the wall along the side of the track. *Never* look at the wall.

Now, if I'm in the driver's seat of that car and starting to lose control, my first thought is going to be a mixture of *Holy Sh*t!* and *Don't hit that wall!* with a little side of *I think I just wet myself.* And all of this, by the way, is happening in a split second. Do you even have *time* to remind yourself not to look at the wall? Probably not. Which is why elite drivers train for years to master the combination of extreme mental focus and complete body relaxation. In a relaxed state, their minds will know what to do and where to focus. Their bodies will naturally follow, regardless of any chaos going on around them. Those are true ninja skills right there.

But *why* is it important not to look at the wall if you're speeding out of control in a race car? Wouldn't you want to know where the wall is so you can avoid hitting it? Quite the opposite. A driver never wants to look at the wall because *the body will follow wherever the mind is focused.* Every time. Focus on the wall, and you're sure to become a human fireball. Focus on the track and where you want the car to go, and you have a much better chance of straightening out your path.

In racing, in business, and in life—your focus determines your results.

When it comes to developing the right mindset for success, it's vital to start with a strong vision that keeps you focused on what you're creating. Focusing on what you don't want, what you fear, or what you wish to avoid will always backfire. This was one of the first lessons I learned in personal development. Your mind doesn't distinguish between "I want" and "I don't want." Thinking *I don't want to hit that wall* is dangerous because your mind will only register the "hit that wall" part.

In your business or passion project, maybe "the wall" for you is your competition or your fear of failure or rejection. Instead of focusing on trying to avoid what you don't want, focus on the situation turning out exactly as you'd like, and you're far more likely to experience your ideal outcome. Your focus determines your results. Let's dive a little deeper into this.

PROGRAMMING YOUR INTERNAL GPS

Remember our earlier conversation about your internal GPS? If you think about it, the GPS feature on your phone is utterly useless unless it has been programmed with a destination. In other words, with a focus. With no direction and no end goal in mind, you'll wind up driving in circles or stuck in the same place.

Your internal GPS is the same, and you program it with your focus. Whatever goal or "destination" you focus on, the GPS will work to help you find the fastest route to get there. Anytime you feel "stuck" or like you're driving in circles—instead of making progress toward your goal—chances are you've lost sight of your destination and it's time to refocus.

Here's the cool thing: when you consistently focus on what you want to create, you'll notice new opportunities show up everywhere. Your internal GPS will always work to find you the fastest route to your destination, or in this case, your goal. You'll even come up with new creative ideas that you hadn't thought of before. Or maybe you'll meet the right person to help you bring your idea to life. All these opportunities, ideas, and people existed all along, but your mind wasn't picking up on them because you weren't programming it to do so. Your internal GPS wasn't set for the correct destination.

If you're starting something new that you've never done before—like a new business or passion project—it can be very easy to slip into worry mode. *Can I really do this? Will I succeed? What will people think if I fail? Do I have what it takes? Will my competition crush me?* Worry is just another way of focusing on exactly what you don't want. And if you are consistently programming your internal GPS for what you don't want, you could end up in a bad neighborhood. With a flat tire. And the hubcaps stripped off your car. Even a powerhouse woman is prone to make a wrong turn every once in a while.

In the middle of this year, my business went through a slow season. I felt like I was putting in the same amount of work, but I wasn't seeing the same returns as I had previously. There are seasons like this in any business. I know that. But this time, instead of viewing my current reality as a normal cycle of business, I started to make it personal. Clearly, I thought there is something wrong with *me* that this is happening. Old internal chatter came rushing back and with a vengeance: *What am I doing wrong? Do I have what it takes to really do this? I suck. I was right all along, I'm not good enough.*

No matter how much personal development I've invested in and no matter how many hours of books and podcasts I listen to, some old habits of the mind are always lurking in the shadows, ready to strike at any moment of weakness. This negative chatter went on inside my head for a few weeks. On the surface, I was doing the same activities I always do, keeping a big smile on my face. Deep down, though, my thoughts had turned to worry, lack, and doubt.

Until something dawned on me—I am focusing on everything I *don't* want, like the people who aren't calling me back, the orders that aren't coming through, the team members who have quit or stopped showing up at training events. These thoughts had crept in very quietly. I justified keeping them around because I couldn't deny the fact that business *had* slowed a bit; I was just acknowledging the current reality, or so I thought. But the more I focused on what wasn't happening, the more I kept getting the same results. My internal GPS had taken a wrong turn into a sketchy neighborhood. There was no space for new creative ideas to appear because I kept reinforcing the current reality that I saw in front of me. I knew that if I wanted to turn things around, I had to start with my focus. And fast.

I started consciously focusing on and speaking about what *was* working. I spent a few minutes every morning reviewing my goals and vision, putting my intention back on what I wanted to *create*, not on what I wanted to avoid. Because some of my old beliefs had crept back in, I knew I needed to dedicate even more energy toward fine-tuning my focus and connecting to my vision for the future. Slowly but surely, my results started to shift, too.

Change never happens immediately. It's the compound effect of consistent thoughts and actions that produce results over time. This means that the results happening for you *now* are a factor of your previous thoughts and actions. In other words, what you think, say, and do today will shape the future results of your business, your life, and your relationships.

The power of focus also comes in handy when dealing with human interaction. It's amazing how differently people can show up in your life simply by changing your focus regarding another person. Let me be clear—nothing about this other person changes. Nothing. You simply change what you're focusing on. Have an annoying family member or coworker? If you keep focusing on what annoys you about the person, you'll continue to find more things to be annoyed about. Notice, however, that if you consciously focus on something you admire, respect, or appreciate about that person, you'll start to see more positive aspects about him or her too.

In relationships, in business, and in life, you'll see more results in whatever area you focus on consistently. The key word here is "consistently"—that is, maintaining steady focus on your goal over an extended period. It's easy to get excited by your initial vision, but the real test will be how disciplined and consistent you can be at maintaining your focus when you encounter the inevitable challenges along the way to your goal. Remember: to bring your big, beautiful vision to life, you've got to guard your focus and consciously shift any worrying back to thoughts about what you *want* to create.

If you're out to do something you've never done before, and you don't know exactly how to get there, you might wonder how you can program that "destination" into your internal GPS. If you don't know exactly what your end goal looks like, you might also wonder how to create a clear picture. The answer lies in a lost art—something children are masterful at, but adults often underestimate: the power of imagination.

MAKE-BELIEVE

My entire childhood was built on make-believe. During the summer, our basement playroom transformed into a schoolhouse, a rainforest, or a royal palace—all depending on the mood my siblings and I were in that day. Sometimes the floor of our living room magically turned into red-hot lava. You had to stay on the furniture (dry land) or one of the pillows strewn around the room (our imaginary boulders), or risk being burned to a crisp. As a child, using my imagination every day was automatic. I never questioned whether any of my creations were plausible or not. I never wondered if talking to an imaginary friend made me look weird. I fully believed in whatever storyline my mind created and acted it out accordingly. When I got bored with one storyline, I created another. I had endless options to choose from. The only limit was my own imagination.

Where, along the way, do adults lose this ability to engage in make-believe? I don't think any of us abandon our imaginary pirate ships intentionally. Becoming more realistic is just a factor of growing up, experiencing some challenging circumstances, and wanting to be more mature. Once it's no longer cool to believe in Santa Claus or the Tooth Fairy, all our imagination can easily get swept into the far back corner of the playroom closet. Make-believe is for naïve little kids, right?

I think your business or passion project would tend to disagree. Make-believe is for grown-ups, too, and it's a powerful way to get your mind on board with where you're going. Why should kids have all the fun? But let me remind you what you'll be dealing with when you start envisioning new goals and dreams. First, your mind *loves* certainty and security, which all ties back to that dang comfort zone again. Second, to your mind, change (which you first create through your imagination) equals DEATH. However, breakthroughs and growth typically happen in the face of *un*certainty. Therefore, to reach your biggest goals, you and your security-seeking mind will need to go somewhere you've never gone, do something you've never done, and be someone you've never been. That kind of challenging uncertainty, if you let it, will scare your mind right back into the playroom closet where it can hide out along with all your old worn-out toys.

Knowing that your mind, at any point, could try hiding out or retreating, it's time to dust off your imagination and give your thoughts a new job and a new destination. To get your mind on board with wherever you're going, you must make any uncertainty seem *less* uncertain. How? By creating a vision of what you want to accomplish as though you've already achieved that vision. In other words, vividly imagine your end goal is a done deal. Just know that whenever you set a goal, your mind will immediately go in search of certainty. And it will usually look to your past for evidence to support its decision-making.

For example, your mind will scan your previous experiences, failures, and successes in search of any evidence that what you're planning to accomplish can or cannot be done. If you're out to do something you've never done before, there's no evidence "on file" for your mind to access. Moving forward without the necessary evidence to calm your certainty-seeking mind is asking for an all-out tug-of-war between your comfort zone and your goal. Therefore, the smarter way to approach taking on a big goal is to solicit the help of your subconscious mind by *planting* the necessary evidence through imagination and visualization.

By vividly imagining your goal as already accomplished, you create a mental map for your brain to follow. You plant the "file" for your mind to reference whenever you go to take action around your new goal. And here's the craziest part, your mind can't tell the difference between something that is *real* and something that has been *vividly and consistently imagined*. To your subconscious mind, it's all the same.

Olympians and elite athletes have been using visualization and mental rehearsal for decades. I've read several pretty cool accounts of elite athletes using visualization to prepare for their sport. In *Mental Training for Peak Performance*, Steven Ungerleider, a sports psychologist, shares numerous examples of Olympic and professional athletes using mental rehearsal as part of their training process. Many athletes consider these visual workouts to be as important as their physical workouts. Before showing up to the main event, the athletes have already run through their specific actions, from beginning to end, hundreds of times in their minds.

A gymnast, for example, will mentally see herself flawlessly performing a floor exercise or balance beam routine from beginning to end. She can feel the gold medal being placed around her neck as she stands proudly on the podium, her country's national anthem playing in the background. A sprinter will visualize her body moving swiftly around the track. She can feel her leg muscles engaging as she passes the other competitors and crosses the finish line in first place. Like these athletes, your mind, too, experiences no difference between performing an activity and vividly imagining it.

The most effective use of your imagination to reach any goal will go beyond visualization to employ all your senses. In other words, the more you're able to see, smell, touch, and feel every aspect of the perfect scenario you're playing out in your mind, the more your mind will believe that it has *already happened*. If your mind believes your goal has already been achieved, you now have "evidence" on file that you can do it again. This is how you enlist the help of your subconscious mind—by planting references of success for your mind to use later.

I use this technique any time I'm preparing to give a presentation. Public speaking is the one thing most people fear more than death. A few years ago, I certainly would have put myself in that category. Even now, I still get butterflies before speaking. Sometimes the butterflies feel more like pterodactyls. But I've taken a page from the Olympians' book and have learned to minimize any performance anxiety through vividly imagining a presentation before I deliver it.

I begin by closing my eyes and mentally bring myself to the stage or room where I'll be speaking. I picture what the room might look like from my vantage point (even if I'm just making it up as I go). I can feel the floor beneath my feet, and I'm taking in the sounds and smells around me. I picture myself making eye contact with the smiling faces in the audience and see them nod in agreement at something I just said. I don't always play out the exact words I plan to say; I'm more focused on anchoring the *feelings* I want to experience in that moment. I'm calm, clearheaded, and articulate. My energy is warm and engaging. I feel connected to the audience and so comfortable it feels as though I'm having a conversation with a close friend. Whatever I want to experience in that moment, I close my eyes and draw up an image of me standing in front of the room, experiencing those exact emotions and body sensations.

By the time I actually stand up to speak, it feels as though I've been in that room in front of those exact people numerous times before. For me, using visualization to mentally rehearse is far more effective than the old advice to "picture the audience in their underwear." There are some things in life you just can't un-see.

Beyond public speaking, you can employ your imagination anywhere in your own business and life. Before an important meeting, close your eyes and visualize it from start to finish. Picture everything going exactly as you want it to. Feel the handshake you receive at the end of the meeting, congratulating you on a new client or business investment you've just gained. If you're a speaker or would like to be, visualize people lining up around the block, just for a chance to hear you speak (even if at the moment speaking in front of an audience of two sounds horrifying). Picture your new best-selling book flying off store shelves. See yourself reading heartfelt testimonials from your ideal clients, sharing how your business or product has changed their life. Imagine what it looks like to go through your day completely tapped into your powerhouse potential. What does that look and feel like for you? If you can imagine it, you can achieve it.

Just to warn you, your grown-up brain *will* try to bring your crazy audacious visions back down to that boring place called "reality." Remember, your mind is always seeking certainty, so you must imagine your intended outcomes consistently and vividly, so that they eventually become "real" to your subconscious mind.

How can you keep your imagined outcomes so present and alive that they start to feel real long before you've accomplished them? By posting them everywhere. And I do mean everywhere. I have notes with my goals posted anywhere and everywhere that I spend a lot of time throughout the day–in my car, next to my desk, all over my office, on my refrigerator, and even on my bathroom mirror. You want to flood your subconscious with a steady stream of evidence that your intended outcome is on its way. Some of the most successful people in the world do this. I once read a story about Jack Canfield, a world-renowned speaker, author, and success coach, putting a picture of a one hundred-thousand-dollar check (his annual income goal at the time) on the ceiling above his bed. It was the first thing he saw in the morning and the last thing he saw at night. In doing this, he was subconsciously telling his mind to keep an eye out for hundred-thousand-dollar ideas. I'd say it worked pretty well for him. Jack now earns many times over his six-figure goal and travels around the world inspiring others.

Another way to keep your vision present is with a vision board, which is essentially a beautiful collage of photos and words to help you keep your goals at the forefront of your mind. I make one at the start of each new year. Over time, it's fun to see how many of the goals I've put on previous vision boards have come true. I always have an old-fashioned vision board with images I've cut out of magazines, but I've also created digital collages that I can save as the background of my computer or phone screen. I don't just look at the pictures, I imagine myself *having* the outcomes I see. I put myself in the scene. The more my subconscious mind is flooded with these images, the easier it is for me to get my mind on board with where I'm headed.

No matter how you choose to keep your mind focused on your goals, the real power of visualization is tapping into the *emotions* and *feelings* that achieving the goal will bring. The more you can vividly picture already having your desired outcome and how it will feel once you accomplish it, the faster you'll achieve it.

STAY PRESENT, FOCUS FORWARD

We'll tie all this talk about focus together with a pretty little bow and one of my favorite daily check-ins. I ask myself these two questions every day (and sometimes multiple times each day): *Am I stretching myself? Am I being present in this moment?* Stretching your limits and focusing forward while also remaining present in the current moment might sound like a contradiction. I've found, however, that combining the two creates the perfect sweet spot for inner peace and massive momentum.

Let's look at the first component, focusing forward and stretching your limits. When you're setting and achieving big goals, there comes a point where you've ventured so far beyond your comfort zone that many different forms of fear can creep in. You might fear whether you'll be able to maintain what you've achieved so far. Or your business could reach a new breakthrough level in sales, and you start to worry about whether you'll be able to sustain that success. Or you sign contracts with a record number of new clients and start to worry about how you'll keep them all happy so they continue doing business with you.

Once you reach any new level, the next and most crucial step is to set a new target that will stretch you *further*. If you don't, it's tempting to start looking at your current result and worrying about how in the world you'll maintain it. And you can guess where worry will lead you—toward attracting the exact outcome you're afraid of. If you're climbing a steep cliff, you want to keep your eyes focused up and toward the destination you're climbing to. Looking down at how far you could fall if you were to let go is a sure way to paralyze yourself with fear.

I see this fear and worry happen all the time in people that I'm working with to cause a breakthrough in their health and fitness. If a person's initial goal is to lose twenty pounds, and they lose it, unless that person sets a new target—maybe around a strength or endurance goal this time—they'll often start to worry about how they'll be able to *maintain* the weight loss and how they'll feel about themselves if they were to put the weight back on. Before they know it, their old habits start to creep back in, and sure enough, the weight starts to pile back on. Without a new stretch target to reach for, the mind will slip into worry. And we've already identified that worry leads to backward progress.

In fitness, your body will go through natural weight fluctuations day-to-day. In business, attrition will happen; products will be returned, and clients will move on. The most successful people in any arena stay focused on where they're going next. When the inevitable attrition happens in my business, for example, I choose to believe that the people who needed to leave will leave, making room for the perfect clients to come in. My focus remains on what I'm attracting next and how I can continue to better support and add value to my existing clients, not on the business that I might have lost.

Keep in mind that focusing on your current results is not the way to move forward. Instead, you must focus forward. Create a bigger game that will force you to become the person who will achieve it. By pursuing this bigger stretch goal, you'll easily maintain the results you've already produced.

You want to create a long-term vision of where you're going, and (here's the second piece of the equation) remain present in the moment with whatever action you're taking.

Here's an example to illustrate what I mean: as an overachiever,

I've always found myself rushing through life—always feeling like I should be doing something else while I'm working on the task at hand. I'll be in the gym, working out, for example, but my mind is already thinking ahead to everything I want to accomplish in my business that day. My body may physically be in the gym doing pull-ups, but my mind is elsewhere. Other times, I'll be sitting at my desk working away, thinking about how I should really get to the gym and work out.

Having my body in one place and my mind in another is exhausting—and completely inefficient, I might add. In contrast, my workouts are much more effective if, while I'm in the gym working out, I'm completely present to what my body is doing. Likewise, my business is far more efficient when, while I'm working on a task, I give my complete and undivided attention to that task until it's complete. I eliminate all distractions, putting my complete focus on my work.

I started the practice of asking myself *Am I being present right now? in the gym? while I'm writing? while I'm talking with someone?* It turns out, I discovered, that although I thought I was "great" at multitasking, I was really just easily distracted and not that focused. Sometimes I'll be writing and notice myself unconsciously opening a web browser and scrolling through Facebook. Ten minutes and some light Internet stalking later, I'm asking myself, *how did I get here?* Distractions can creep in and steal my focus away far too easily.

Being present is a moment-by-moment awareness—something you'll always be working on improving. Just like the Indy car driver who works to master the combination of extreme mental focus and complete body relaxation, your goal as a business owner is to master the combination of thinking big about the future while being present.

In other words, allow yourself to be pulled forward by your big vision and stretch goals but remain completely present and focused in your day-to-day execution of those goals.

My biggest takeaway from this chapter:

LET'S RECAP

- Your mind can't tell the difference between something that's real and something that has been vividly and consistently imagined. Therefore, your imagination can be a powerful tool to use in creating a blueprint for success for your mind to follow.

- The best use of imagination and visualization is to engage all your senses. Feel the feelings that the achievement of your goal will bring.

- Your focus determines your results, so focus on what you want to create, not what you want to avoid.

- Your internal GPS will always work to find the fastest route to the destination it's programmed for. You program your GPS by what you focus on.

- The sweet spot for massive momentum in your business or passion project is to have a big vision for the future that pulls you forward while remaining completely present to the task at hand.

POWERHOUSE ACTION PLAN:
PROGRAM YOUR INTERNAL GPS FOR SUCCESS

Over the next few days, start to become aware of your focus. If you've never paid attention to what your mind focuses on throughout the day, this can be an extremely eye-opening experience in the best way. A simple shift in focus can produce a huge difference in your results. In the following chapters, we'll build on the principle of focus and start to specifically tune your awareness for maximum success. For now, the goal is to bring awareness to your current focus.

Your first challenge is to bring awareness to what you focus on throughout the day.

For one entire day, check in periodically and simply notice what your mind is focused on. You could set an alarm on your phone, alerting you every hour or two to check your focus. When the alert pops up, just notice what you are focused on in that moment. Is your mind focused on the task at hand, or are you thinking about something you need to do later? Are you worrying about something that you can't directly control in the moment? Whatever you notice, don't judge yourself for it. The purpose is to bring awareness. Use the space below to record what you noticed from taking on this exercise for one full day.

Think about one area of your business, passion project, or life where you aren't currently experiencing the results you want. Be honest and ask yourself, what have I been focused on in this area? *Examples: I'm focusing on how many people haven't returned my phone calls. I'm worried about how I'll maintain my current clients. I'm focused on the lack of results I currently see. I'm comparing myself to the success I see others having. I'm thinking about how I'm not doing enough to achieve my goals.*

I'm sure you do spend a good chunk of time focusing on what you do want in this area, but if it truly isn't working the way you'd like at the moment, then chances are some sneaky thoughts of doubt or lack may have snuck in without you noticing. Tuning your awareness to these thoughts gives you immediate access to change them. And when you change your focus, you change your results and your life.

What is one area where I can see I'm ready to stretch myself further and set a bigger target or goal to work toward?

What is a stretch goal in this area?

POWER #6:
EMBRACE RESISTANCE

Whenever you're taking on a new challenge or growing to the next level, it's only a matter of time before you encounter resistance. Resistance is an integral part of growth. It's inevitable. Your mindset and attitude will play a huge role in determining how powerfully you're able to operate while in the resistance phase. The question isn't *Will I encounter resistance*, but rather, *How will I choose to respond in the face of it?*

Have you ever had one of those dreams where you're trying to run away from something or someone, yet no matter how hard you try, you can't move any faster than a snail's pace? It's as though your legs are made of solid concrete. Every movement requires ten times the energy and strength it normally would. You're watching everything around you move at normal speed, but you're operating in super slo-mo.

In my experience, that's exactly what resistance feels like.

Resistance can be physically and mentally draining. By stepping into your power and pursuing your nudge, you are essentially challenging your current identity to a wrestling match. Everything within you is fighting to maintain homeostasis and remain comfortable, but your nudge is begging you to grow. The wrestling match that ensues is the resistance phase.

Resistance can come from outside of you in the form of a challenge or obstacle that threatens to derail your progress. It can also come from within. You may physically feel yourself avoiding certain opportunities, situations, and actions, as if every fiber of your being is resisting your own growth. Your inner critic loves to chime in when you're facing resistance. It's a great opportunity for her to throw a jab or two because you're typically more vulnerable.

What exactly triggers resistance? Any change or growth, really. It could be the discomfort of growing to a new level of personal success and struggling to break through old habits. Maybe you experience the growing pains of finding and hiring the right partners to help bring your nudge to life. Or it could be the challenges of expanding into a new market, launching a new product, or stretching the smallest of budgets to fund your big dreams.

Even success can bring resistance. Your business grows too fast, and you're faced with logistical issues. Maybe you feel pulled in a million different directions. Or you experience a surge of success and suddenly feel overcome with a gripping fear about whether you'll be able to maintain your success. Good or bad, resistance can paralyze you. A resistance phase is often accompanied by feelings of discomfort, anxiety, or frustration. On a personal level, sometimes when I'm bumping up against my next breakthrough, I'll notice that I feel physically exhausted for no reason at all. It's as if everything within me is fighting the growth I'm going through.

How you respond in the face of resistance will make a big difference in the speed at which you reach your goals. There's also a common theme in how successful people view resistance. They not only expect and anticipate the phenomenon; they often seek it out, viewing resistance as not only inevitable, but desirable. Because when you break it down, resistance is just evidence of a gap between where you are now and where you want to go. That gap is your opportunity to grow.

In fact, the gap is necessary for you to grow.

Think of it this way. If you go to the gym and lift weights with the intention of getting stronger—let's say you're doing a bicep curl—what would happen if you set the weights down the moment you feel the slightest amount of discomfort, the moment you encounter resistance? Would your muscle ever grow or become stronger? Not a chance! In fact, the whole purpose of lifting weights isn't to *build* the muscle. The purpose is to *tear it down* so that your body rebuilds a bigger, stronger muscle in its place. You need the resistance to put tension on the muscle and create microscopic tears in the tissue. When this happens, then your body can go to work using the protein you consume to rebuild the muscle into one that can handle that amount of resistance next time. The muscle won't grow unless it faces resistance. Neither will you, and neither will your business.

Knowing at a logical level that resistance is fundamentally good and that it's refining you to fulfill your purpose is one thing, but *operating powerfully* while you're in the middle of the experience is another. Resistance can take on a multitude of different forms, and there's too many for us to cover them all. But I want to dive deeper into two specific forms of resistance that I think threaten the pursuit of your nudge the most. It is critical for you to be able to distinguish both scenarios as exactly what they are—a form of resistance. If you know you're in resistance, you now have a choice to move through it, which is exactly what we'll talk about at the end of this lesson: how to keep moving forward when you find yourself in any form of resistance.

PERFECTIONISM

Do you ever shake your head when looking back at some of the things your twenty-something-year-old self said or did? If you are currently still in your twenties, you may not yet be at this point, but, trust me, it's coming. One of my particularly head-shake inducing memories is of sitting in job interviews as a soon-to-be college grad. Optimistic about the future and totally clueless about what adult life is really like, I heard this question in almost every interview: "What would you say is your biggest weakness?" My entire life up to this point was pretty much designed around concealing any shortcomings, so I'd pretend to ponder the question for a moment and reply with my perfectly curated and canned response: "Well, I'm a pretty big perfectionist."

Oh, please. Such a cop-out response, I know. Would all of the stereotypical first-born overachievers please stand up? This answer itself reeked of my desire to portray an inauthentic image of having everything together. Which, let's be real, no one does. The sad thing is that I naively saw my "perfectionism" as more of a strength than a weakness. The answer was a cover-up for the truth that I was unable and unwilling to face: I was terrified of failure; therefore, I pretty much avoided all risk. In reality, avoiding risk would have been a legitimate weakness when it comes to being a qualified job candidate, but I didn't know that at the time. Oh, how much I still had to learn about the "real world" and the value of being authentic for myself and with other people.

I wish I could say that I grew out of my perfectionist tendencies as I became older and wiser. It hasn't quite been that easy. In many ways, I'm still the classic first-born overachiever. I still allow perfectionism to distract me from my purpose on occasion. At least now though, I can recognize perfectionism as one of the most dangerous forms of resistance and one of the greatest threats to a nudge. Perfectionism inherently shuns growth because to admit that there is even room for growth would be admitting a lack of perfection. If resistance is the gap between where you are now and where you want to go—the only way through that gap is imperfect growth.

I still have high standards for the work that I do, and I'm proud of that. I've learned, however, that there's a big difference between having high standards and being a self-defeating perfectionist. High standards and perfection might sound similar, but perfectionism is just procrastination dressed in a fancy outfit. Perfectionism can stall progress by strapping a big heavy ball and chain around your ankle, making it nearly impossible to leave your current comfort zone and risk looking foolish or imperfect in pursuit of a nudge.

Maybe you don't identify with full-on perfectionism, but do you ever set completely unrealistic expectations for yourself? I do. In my business, in my fitness goals, and around the kind of mother I will be (and I don't even have children yet!). I could go on. By creating impossible-to-achieve standards, I set myself up to be overwhelmed. This, in turn, becomes the perfect excuse for not getting anything done. It's okay to notice yourself in a similar pattern, just don't hang out there for too long.

The way to move through this type of resistance when you notice yourself in expectation overwhelm is to allow yourself to suck. Yes, I said it. It's perfectly normal to suck at something in the beginning. In fact, you should expect it. If you're going from one nudge to the next, following where your curiosities lead you, you will often have the experience of being a newbie. And the only way a newbie becomes a pro is by going through the necessary learning curve to develop pro-level skills, beliefs, and habits. But, in the beginning, most newbies will suck.

The people we admire for being great at what they do were all beginners at one point. Every professional athlete had the day they first picked up a volleyball, tennis racket, or hockey stick. For every business success, an investor experiences countless failures. Even people with natural talents must hone their craft for years before they are ever recognized as legendary. We don't see the countless hours of time poured into repeating the same steps over and over again until they've mastered their expertise. It may not be the sexy stuff, but mastering the mundane and the willingness to suck before you excel is essential to move through this type of resistance.

If this is the first business you've ever started, or if you're making a sharp left turn into an industry or profession that you have little experience in, there will be a learning curve. You'll be a bit of a hot mess before you're a total success. Think about it this way, people spend anywhere from two to four (or more) years getting a college degree or technical training before they ever start working in their chosen profession. You wouldn't expect to walk in the first day of school and have completely mastered your chosen trade, would you? You wouldn't expect to be paid as a twenty-year veteran of your profession the first day as an intern, right? The beginning phase of any new project is like going back to school, except when we're adults, it's easy to forget which phase we're in and expect to be a rock star Day One. Any expectation on the contrary is just resistance, threatening to stop you before you ever get started.

Repeat after me: "It's okay to suck."

IMPOSTER SYNDROME

If you're able to free yourself from the grasp of perfectionism and venture out into the unknown, you're likely to encounter another form of resistance at some point—imposter syndrome. Just a few weeks ago I was reading an article in *Success* magazine about Sophia Amoruso, founder of the wildly successful *Nasty Gal* brand, author of the bestselling book *#Girlboss*, and one of *Forbes* richest self-made women. If you don't know anything about her background, let's just say she wasn't exactly voted most likely to succeed. Before starting her first vintage fashion eBay store, the one that would later evolve into the *Nasty Gal* empire that exists today, her experiences ranged from hitchhiking and working odd jobs to dumpster diving and petty theft. Not exactly the résumé you'd expect from someone who would go on to create a fashion empire and accumulate an estimated net worth of $280 million.

As I was reading the *Success* article, one thing jumped off the page. Amoruso said that she felt like an imposter, pretending to be someone she wasn't, at certain points along the way to building her massive empire. My first thought was, "Wait, successful people feel like that too?" It turns out, they do.

Do you ever feel like an imposter, like your current identity doesn't quite match the big vision you have for your future? I sure as hell do, and lately it's a solid 95 percent of the time. But ever since I first started pursuing my nudge, I have learned that it's *good* to feel out of your league. Imposter syndrome, like any form of resistance, is an opportunity to grow and expand your current comfort zone.

Knowing that it's a good thing to feel totally uncomfortable and out of my league doesn't make me *like* the feeling any more than I previously did. But I'll admit, hearing that a total powerhouse like Sophia Amoruso also feels like an imposter from time to time was oddly comforting. All of a sudden I was a whole lot less self-conscious about my own feelings of inadequacy. I started to clearly see that along the path of building my business and pursuing my nudge, the times when I felt most like an imposter were also the times when I grew the most.

When I first started my health and fitness business, I can vividly remember how uncomfortable it felt to answer the simple question of what I did for a living. I had gone from a corporate career selling commercial flooring to my own independent business, coaching people to achieve their health and fitness goals—not exactly a logical career transition, so my inner critic was having none of it.

I started attending networking events, totally intimidated and out of my comfort zone, but willing to do whatever was necessary in pursuit of my nudge. My palms would sweat as everyone took turns standing up and sharing what they did for a living and what their ideal client referral looked like. A lot of the individuals had been working in their fields for longer than I had been alive. When my turn came, I would semi black out but manage to utter something to the effect of "I'm a healthy lifestyle coach." Without missing a beat, my inner critic would chime in. *Who YOU? No, you're not.*

I persisted despite how incredibly uncomfortable I felt speaking up at these events. Eventually, my inner critic's opinions on the matter weren't as deafening. The more I practiced, the better I got at explaining what I did and how I could provide value for people. As I grew, I started to see my business grow. Now, after over six years of building a successful business, I have a totally different posture around what I do. The increased confidence only multiplies my results, but I wouldn't have gotten to this point had I not been willing to feel like a total imposter first.

Fast forward to January 2016 when I decided to take on the challenge of writing a book, something totally new and waaaayyyy out of my comfort zone. My inner critic has had a field day with this one. *Who are you to write a book? You're not that successful. What can you contribute to anyone? Other people are already doing what you want to do and doing it better.*

The sound of my resistance has been almost audible, especially as I get closer to completing my manuscript, which shouldn't be surprising because resistance will often feel the strongest the closer you are to a breakthrough. So if you are feeling the tension of resistance around something important to you right now, remember that it's a lot like the feeling of pressure building up in your ears while ascending to cruising altitude in an airplane. The pressure feels the greatest right before you feel the blissful *pop* of relief.

The resistance of imposter syndrome will often come on the heels of a comparison to someone who is further along than you are. Of course, you'll always feel like an imposter standing next to a person you look up to. Remember, though, the person you look up to probably feels like an imposter too, especially compared to someone further along the journey than they are. The dire need for people to pursue their unique nudge is far greater than the number of people currently answering the call. There is room for each and every voice because no one person can relate to every human being. Stay in your own lane, focus on the people you feel called to serve, and trust that when your message is clear, your tribe will find you. They're just waiting for you to step up and let them know you're here.

With every new level of my own achievement, I've had the nagging feeling that I'm totally out of my league, along with the fear that I'm pretending to be something I'm not (and it's only a matter of time before someone calls me out). When I face imposter syndrome head-on and continue to put myself in situations where I'm totally out of my league, I always grow and get to experience just how capable I really am.

"It's good to feel out of your league. You should try to spend most of your time feeling out of your league, because then you'll grow into it and find another league."
—Sophia Amoruso

BE LIKE THE BUFFALO

When it comes to any form of resistance, I've found that three things help me move powerfully through it and grow in the process. First, remember that your nudge (and ultimately your business or passion project) is not about you. It's 100 percent about who you are meant to serve. Any suffering you experience because of resistance is typically a sign that you're focusing on yourself, not on serving others. A powerhouse woman maintains a positive attitude and remembers that resistance is a necessary part of growth.

Second, remember that your focus determines your results. When you experience resistance, focus forward on your vision, not on the resistance itself. Acknowledge that resistance is a necessary part of pursuing your nudge and that it means you are growing. Then turn your focus to what's waiting on the other side of that growth.

Third, and the most important thing to remember about moving through resistance, be like the buffalo. Let me explain. I've heard several accounts of how buffalo respond to resistance in the wild. One of the greatest threats buffalo face hanging out in the open plains is the weather. When a storm rolls in, instead of turning and trying to outrun the wind and rain, a herd of buffalo will actually run into the storm, charging toward the discomfort and resistance. By running through bad weather, buffalo shorten the amount of time they spend in a storm.

What can you learn about resistance from the buffalo? Any time you try to avoid or outrun resistance, you inevitably end up prolonging it. By avoiding the phone calls you're uncomfortable making, by avoiding a difficult conversation because you don't like confrontation, or by avoiding the gym because you don't feel like you know what you're doing, you delay the breakthrough waiting for you. When you avoid what's uncomfortable, you prolong your own learning curve. In contrast, the more you seek out and press into your resistance, the more you'll grow. And growth, at the end of the day, is what pursuing your nudge is all about.

My biggest takeaway from this chapter:

LET'S RECAP

- Resistance is inevitable when pursuing something you've never done. It's evidence of the gap between where you are now and where you want to go.
- Your attitude and mindset will play a big role in determining how long you stay in the resistance phase.
- Resistance can be a very good thing for you and your business if you choose to see it that way.
- It's okay to suck. When going from nudge to nudge and following your curiosities, you will often experience being a newbie.
- Any successful person has felt like an imposter at first. It's good to feel out of your league. That's how you grow.
- To powerfully move forward in the face of resistance, be like the buffalo. Run toward, not away from, the storm.

POWERHOUSE ACTION PLAN:
RUN TOWARD RESISTANCE

What is something you can see you have been unwilling to "suck" at? What are you not trying or doing because you won't be good at it yet?

Describe any ways you have felt like an imposter in pursuing your nudge.

What is one uncomfortable thing that you know you've been resisting something that would cause you to grow? *Examples: avoiding a difficult conversation, not attending networking functions, putting off making sales calls, delaying scheduling a first event.*

I dare you! *Complete one of the actions you've been resisting within the next 48 hours.*

POWER #7:
PLUG INTO GRATITUDE

If there were a magic pill that would not only improve your overall well-being and help you sleep better, but would also make you happier, improve all your relationships (including your own self-image), and positively impact your business, would you take it? Well, a growing body of research supports the theory that this "magic cure" actually exists, and it's been available to you all along. Best of all, it's completely free.

I'm talking about Vitamin G—gratitude.

Now, if you've invested in a lot of personal development like I have, this isn't some radical new conversation. Gratitude is a widely discussed topic that, in my opinion, can never be discussed too much. It's absolutely at the core of a well-rounded success mindset. Let's take a deeper look at some aspects of gratitude you may not be practicing regularly, and, as a result, how you may be unintentionally sabotaging your own success.

In his book *Thanks!: How Practicing Gratitude Can Make You Happier*, Robert A. Emmons, Ph.D., a leading gratitude psychology researcher, demonstrates that expressing gratitude has the potential to increase overall happiness by as much as 25 percent. *Twenty-five percent!* Just by tuning into thoughts of gratitude. In another one of his studies, participants kept a daily written record of what they were most grateful for, and they reported not only better sleep but increased energy levels as well.

But the true power of gratitude goes beyond the words "thank you." All the power lies in the emotion and energy behind gratitude. Expressing gratitude in words without feeling grateful is like plugging your cell phone charger into a wall with no electric current running through it. You're not connecting to the power source that gratitude can provide for your life. I will grant that the words and feelings of gratitude don't always go hand in hand. Have you ever said "thank you" out of habit? The supermarket cashier hands you your change, and the words automatically fall out of your mouth, more as a reflex than a true expression of gratitude.

Contrast this scenario with a thank you paired with emotion—the kind of gratitude you might experience if a doctor just performed a lifesaving surgery on the person you love most. In the case of the supermarket cashier, a simple thank you is appropriate. It might be a little awkward if you reach across the checkout counter for a hug with tears welling up in your eyes upon receiving a handful of change, but you get the point.

When you tap into the feelings and emotions of gratitude, you supercharge its power.

One way to cultivate the deeper *feelings* of gratitude is to zone in on specific things you are grateful for. Get clear on exactly how whatever you're expressing gratitude for actually impacts your life. Like anyone, I know I take a lot of things in my life for granted daily: access to healthy food and clean water, a house with air conditioning that protects me from the Arizona heat, a reliable vehicle, a healthy body, a warm bed . . . the list goes on. While I could use the blanket statement that "I'm grateful for my life," which is absolutely true, getting specific about what I'm most grateful for (and imagining how different my life would be without clean water, food, or shelter) gives me access to the deeper emotions of my gratitude.

Gratitude is also a powerful antidote for any negative emotion, and a powerhouse woman takes complete responsibility for the emotions she chooses to experience. If you think about it, it's *really* difficult to be grateful and upset at the same time. Gratitude is at the opposite end of the emotional spectrum from anger, frustration, envy, or sadness, making it nearly impossible for any of these negative emotions to coexist in the same moment that you are feeling grateful. When I find myself in any emotional pattern that I don't want, my quickest access to reconnect with my power is through gratitude.

We all go through periods of frustration or anger. Life doesn't always go our way. But there is so much power in realizing that we have control over how long we choose to stay in any negative emotional space. We have the power to change how we feel in any moment, all the time. I've found gratitude to be the most powerful tool to help me make that change. At the end of this lesson, I've included some easy ways to create a daily habit of gratitude. But first, let's take a closer look at how gratitude can impact three of the most important areas of your life—your relationships, your health, and your business or passion project.

GRATITUDE AND YOUR RELATIONSHIPS

Not only does gratitude have a positive impact on you, it can also be especially powerful in your relationships, both personally and professionally. Gratitude completely changed many of my relationships for the better, especially my marriage. My husband Elliot is the first guy I've ever lived with. To say that the first few months were an adjustment is an understatement. Who am I kidding? We've now been married six years, and I feel like I'm *still* learning new things every day about how two imperfect people can peacefully cohabitate. Sharing closet space, the stereotypical toilet seat up-or-down debate, and my biggest area of frustration—our very different definitions of the word *clean*. I'll let you take a wild guess which one of us is the neat freak. In our first year of marriage, I just couldn't understand how we could be looking at the exact same kitchen and see two completely different rooms. I zoomed in on the crumbs on the floor, the dishes piled high in the sink, and the scattered pieces of mail randomly covering the dining table *(Really? We couldn't put these in a neat little pile or something?)*. Elliot thought the kitchen looked completely fine. Same kitchen, two radically different views.

Even when I didn't express my frustration out loud, I'm pretty sure he picked up on my snotty attitude as I rearranged the dishwasher he had just loaded so it would meet *my* standards. Yeah, I'm *that* girl. Thankfully, I realized early on in our marriage that I had an important choice to make. I could spend the next fifty years picking him apart for how differently he prioritized cleanliness, believing my way was the "right" way, or I could consciously choose to focus on the qualities that I'm most grateful for in my husband—the things about Elliot that I could never imagine my life without.

Now don't get me wrong. I still have meltdown moments. I don't have this gratitude thing handled, not by any stretch of the imagination. But when I do make the conscious choice to focus on gratitude, it's amazing how much *more* I notice all the best things about my husband and how much he contributes to our home. Without me asking, he takes out the garbage. He stops me in the middle of the kitchen for an impromptu slow dance, like he stepped right out of a flipping rom com. And he makes me laugh. Like, all the time. Elliot works extremely hard, has the kindest heart, and always sees the best in people. And, most important, he doesn't judge me for rearranging the dishwasher that he just loaded, which, in and of itself, should qualify him for a Nobel Peace Prize.

When I focus on what I'm most grateful for, I immediately tap into my love for him. Those crumbs on the kitchen floor magically fade into the background.

Gratitude is like a superhighway to a state of love.

When I'm focused on a complaint, however, our relationship can turn into a dramatic snowball of pent-up frustration that eventually boils over into an unnecessary fight. Now here's the cool thing about all this: I'm the one in control of which state I choose to spend the majority of my time in—love or frustration. I always have the opportunity to seek out and express gratitude for my husband, regardless of what's happening at that moment (messy kitchen and all). And so do you.

Now let's apply gratitude to business relationships. The truth is, for most of us, business involves working with people who we don't always see eye to eye with. I believe that gratitude is one of the most powerful antidotes to frustrations or complaints about a person. See if you can find one thing to be grateful for in that moment. Not just for the other person's benefit, but mainly for *your* benefit. Tapping into gratitude mentally frees you from the grips of anger or irritation, allowing you to think more clearly and creatively. To do any of this though, you first have to be willing to see the situation differently—without the other person changing anything. You hold responsibility for the emotions you experience in any moment, and you can choose to change them by what you focus on.

You can also practice gratitude in your relationships proactively. If you want to see an increase in productivity at work and home, start sprinkling gratitude around like confetti. Seek out opportunities to genuinely acknowledge people in your life for the great things they do. (Yes, even if you feel like they are only doing what you expected them to do.) Take the time to personally thank your friends, employees, clients, or business associates. You're likely to start seeing *more* to be grateful for in these relationships. Chances are the people in your life will also like being around you a whole lot more, too.

GRATITUDE AND YOUR BODY

Gratitude can also have a major impact in your relationship with yourself, specifically, with your own body. As powerhouse women, this relationship is important to talk about because I believe that being at war with yourself and your body is a huge distraction from pursuing your purpose. It's inauthentic for us to be working in the world to promote love, acceptance, and prosperity through our businesses, while on the inside, insulting ourselves and our bodies, the beautiful vessels that allow us to carry out our purpose.

I want you to imagine for a moment that you just turned sixteen. You receive the most amazing birthday gift of all time, something every sixteen-year-old has her heart set on—a car. Now before you get too excited and hit the streets belting *Don't Stop Believing* at the top of your lungs, there's one small catch. Your parents tell you that this is the one and only car you will ever own for the rest of your life. Knowing this, how well would you take care of it? Would you change the oil regularly? Keep it clean and well maintained?

Would you fill the tank with only the most premium fuel? How much would you appreciate having a vehicle to take you where you want to go?

Maybe you see where I'm going here. It's ironic how easily we grasp the concept of care and maintenance when it comes to a vehicle, yet when it comes to our own bodies—the only "vehicle" you'll ever travel around this earth in—all that knowledge and perspective quickly goes out the window. Many of us, myself included, take our bodies and health for granted at times, especially when we're young. We focus heavily on outward appearances over internal well-being, easily shoving self-care and preventative maintenance to the bottom of our priority list, the busier life gets. What if we shifted the context of health to one of gratitude? What would it look like to eat, move, and speak in a way that shows love and appreciation for our bodies rather than a desire to fix or change something? Gratitude can totally shift the paradigm of health and fitness.

I've had my fair share of struggles with self-image. And it doesn't take much to trigger a thought of what I'd love to fix or change about my body. Some days I'll look in the mirror and see a fit, beautiful woman smiling back. Other times I'll notice myself zooming in on my perceived flaws and entertaining that old persistent conversation of *not enough*. I'll put on a pair of jeans one day and radiate confidence. Then the very next day the same pair of jeans seem to highlight every part of my anatomy that I'd prefer to minimize. Nothing about my body changed overnight; any flaws I perceive are completely a product of my thoughts and internal dialogue—two things I have the power to change, if I choose. Working in health and fitness for the better part of the past decade has given me a valuable perspective on the relationship between gratitude and body image. I've come to learn that no matter how much I help someone transform their outer self, if a woman's inner dialogue is still overrun by thoughts of self-criticism, no outward change will ever be enough to make her happy. True transformation must start within.

The law of focus applies here, too. We'll always get more of what we focus on. I firmly believe that if you go the gym and work out, but then you come home, and for the remaining twenty-three hours of the day, proceed to silently insult your body with thoughts like *My thighs are fat, I'm not thin enough*, or *Oh my gosh, look at all these wrinkles*, it's just as counterproductive to being healthy and fit as devouring an entire pizza and two-liter bottle of Coke.

Insulting thoughts about your body will reinforce exactly what you don't want.

The source of our power as women is holistic, encompassing our mind, body, and soul. Unleashing your inner powerhouse starts with reconnecting to self-love. If there is a void in your heart that only self-love can fill, then no amount of outward success will ever be enough. Ignoring the void or pretending it doesn't matter will only lessen the impact you're able—and destined—to make.

I know it's no easy feat to go from a lifetime of self-judgement immediately into self-love. I'm still a work in progress too, but that's where gratitude comes in. Just as with relationships, gratitude can be a superhighway to love. In this case, *self-love*. If you aren't able to admit what you *love* about your body, start with finding gratitude for all that your body does for you on a daily basis. Think about all the bones and muscles in your feet and legs, as well as the brain signals necessary for you to take a simple step. Think about the veins that carry blood from your heart to your extremities and the ears that allow you to hear your favorite song or a child laughing. Think about all the complex body functions that are being used even now, to allow you to read the words on this page. Our bodies are an absolute miracle.

Maybe you don't personally struggle with this type of love/hate relationship with your body, but you probably know at least a dozen women who do. Together, we can start to change the conversation for all of humanity and create change for the next generation of women who are watching our every move and listening to everything we say. We can never expect young women to love themselves and fiercely pursue their own path if we aren't setting an empowering example.

GRATITUDE AND YOUR BUSINESS OR PASSION PROJECT

Several months ago when my business went through a temporary slow season, I quickly realized that I was only reinforcing the slowdown by focusing on exactly what I *didn't* want. The fastest way I've found to redirect a misguided focus—around my relationships, health, or business—is through gratitude. You're probably starting to notice a theme here. Gratitude is a high-vibe energy frequency. Think of it like a giant magnet. Gratitude will naturally attract other high-vibe people, situations, and circumstances into your path. Other high-vibe energy frequencies include success and abundance, things you would naturally want for your business or passion project. In contrast, thoughts of worry, doubt, fear, and lack are all low-vibe frequencies.

Infusing your business or passion project with gratitude is vital, both in good times and growing times. One way to unintentionally cut off the flow of success in your business is by not being grateful for the results you currently have, whether big or small. Have you ever caught yourself saying something like, "Well I'm only making x amount," or "I only have three clients"? The subtle addition of the word *only* completely diminishes the accomplishments you've had thus far, and that one word communicates a lack of gratitude for the results you currently have.

Especially as a new business owner, it's easy to downplay the crucial first steps of the journey in the desire to go right from zero to one hundred. But here is one of the most crucial lessons I've learned in business—you cannot expect to receive more abundance and success if you aren't grateful for the amount you currently have. You will *always* have a bigger vision for where you see your business in the future. There is absolutely nothing wrong with that, and by no means am I telling you to lose your drive to succeed. Being content is not the same as being complacent. There's a fine balance between clearly seeing a picture of what the future will look like, all while operating from a place of gratitude in every baby step along the path. Finding and maintaining that balance is the sweet spot where everything in your business starts to flow.

A powerful way to start tuning into the high-vibe frequency of success and abundance is to look for every little opportunity to express and experience gratitude. Say "thank you" for every dollar of revenue generated by your business and actually pause to appreciate it. Instead of minimizing the small incremental wins you have, celebrate them the same as if you just closed the biggest deal of your career. Acknowledge people every single chance you get. I can't emphasize this enough. Most people in the world are starving for recognition and acknowledgement. A simple text or hand-written note to express appreciation for your employees, business partners, or clients is virtually free and takes less than five minutes, but these gestures of gratitude leave an invaluable impact.

If you ever find yourself focused on what you don't want or on the results that aren't happening (like I did earlier this year), interrupt the negative energy by sprinkling gratitude around like confetti. Wild appreciation will not only create change in your heart and open you up to new ideas, but it creates a positive ripple effect in the world that can last a lifetime. Taking the focus off yourself and pouring love into others is the quickest way to reconnect with what your nudge is all about in the first place.

Hint . . . it's not about you.

The other way to infuse your business with gratitude is through generosity. I've learned a huge lesson about the power of generosity over the last two years. In the past, I always felt the need to control and protect things, especially money. I didn't see money the same way I do now, as energy. Energy is meant to *flow* and circulate. If you hold on to energy, it becomes stagnant. One of the worst things for your business or passion project is stagnant energy.

It's not that I wasn't generous at all, but I always gave from whatever was leftover once my expenses were met. If there wasn't anything leftover, I didn't give. When I started to see money as a tool, a resource, and, ultimately, energy, it freed me up to start letting go. And not in a careless way—quite the opposite. With my husband, who is also my business partner, we sat down and reworked our budget. Only this time, we prioritized giving *first*. We designated the first ten percent of everything we earned as the starting point for what we were committed to giving. We chose to give to our church. If giving is something you're considering, you can, of course, contribute to whatever cause or organization you feel drawn to. The key is to give from a generous heart.

Let me be clear: my husband and I weren't rolling in dough at this point. We had a substantial credit card debt that we were working diligently to pay off. We also had very little savings. It felt tempting to prioritize our other financial goals before we started giving, but I've come to learn that the best time to give is when you don't think you have enough. Giving before you feel like you're in a financial position to do so is an act of trust. Generosity shows that you see money as a tool to be used for good, not an object to control and hold onto.

The first few times we got a paycheck, I sat down to write a donation check for the week that was bigger than we would typically give for an entire month. That size of donation felt a little uncomfortable. Over the following weeks and months, I could feel my faith being stretched, but my tight grasp of control also started to loosen. When we sat down to look over our taxes in December that year, after a full year of putting generosity first, I could hardly believe the numbers staring back at me. Not only did we give more than we had ever given in a single year, but our total income grew by more than *double* the amount we gave. I can't make this up; the numbers didn't lie.

I don't share any of this with you to boast about our generosity or as a strategy to grow your business. Generosity and gratitude aren't guaranteed to produce any monetary return. The purpose of generosity is to put your heart—and the heart of your business—in the right place. When your heart is in the right place, you get yourself out of the way so miracles can happen.

LET THE GRATITUDE CONFETTI FLY

The positive impact of gratitude goes far beyond your relationships, your body, and your business. I look at gratitude like brushing my teeth—for best results, express gratitude daily. Even if you aren't totally sold on the idea, what do you have to lose? I can promise you one thing: incorporating more gratitude in your life won't ever make things worse.

A few suggestions for how you can start practicing gratitude daily:

- Keep a gratitude journal and write out ten items of gratitude every day. Instead of recycling the obvious ones, challenge yourself to come up with a fresh new list of ten every day. After a while, you'll be forced to get really creative. I've written gratitude for everything from my limbs, to my digestion, to my brain's ability to quickly calculate a 33 percent discount on a pair of killer shoes. Focusing on tiny blessings you're surrounded by daily quickly cures any funky mood.

- When eating a meal with a group of people—friends, family, even coworkers—take a few minutes to go around and have each person at the table share one thing they are grateful for. They may look at you funny when you first suggest it, but doing so powerfully changes the energy in the room. You'll be surprised how much it shifts the whole dinner conversation. Do this with kids too, either at meals or bed time, and teach 'em young about the power of gratitude!

- Schedule time in your calendar each week to focus on and express gratitude. It might sound stupid to schedule gratitude, but if you're anything like me, what doesn't get scheduled doesn't get done. Have some fun with it! Find a creative way to feature a great client or employee on your social media channels. Schedule time to make three personal phone calls each week with the sole intent to acknowledge someone in your life.

- Send a handwritten "thank you" card. Yes, the real kind that you mail with a stamp. Who doesn't love receiving *real* mail that isn't a bill? You could start the practice of sending them to your clients, to friends, or to people in your life who least expect it. Secret ninja gratitude is often the most fun. You may be doing it to brighten their day, but you'll be surprised how much it brightens yours too!

- For an entire day, consciously replace complaints with gratitude. Instead of complaining about your messy house, take a moment to let it sink in how blessed you are to have a home, a safe shelter with running water and plumbing. If you catch yourself thinking anything insulting about your own body, switch your thoughts to gratitude for all that your body does for you. Every time a complaint crosses your mind or slips past your lips, rewind and replace it with gratitude. Make it a game with yourself to see how quickly you can catch the complaint and reframe it.

- Leave an extra big tip and a note of gratitude for the server during your next meal out. I can share from first-hand experience that serving can be a thankless job. The minimum wage for servers can be far below the actual minimum wage.

- Perform random acts of kindness. Mow a neighbor's lawn, pay for a stranger's coffee, or make dinner for a family in need. You don't always have to express generosity monetarily either. Giving your time and energy is another way to express your gratitude.

My biggest takeaway from this chapter:

LET'S RECAP

- The true power of gratitude lies in the feelings and emotions associated with it.
- To tap into the emotions of gratitude, focus on specific things you are grateful for. The more specific, the better.
- Gratitude is also a powerful antidote for any negative emotion—anger, frustration, envy, or sadness.
- The fastest way to redirect a misguided focus—around your relationships, health, or business—is through expressing gratitude.
- You always have control of which emotional state you choose to spend the majority of your time in.
- Gratitude is like a superhighway to love.
- Being at war with yourself and your body is a huge distraction from pursuing your purpose.
- One way to unintentionally cut off the flow of success in your business is by not being grateful for the results you currently have, whether big or small.
- Generosity is a powerful way to connect with gratitude.

POWERHOUSE ACTION PLAN:
CULTIVATE AN ATTITUDE OF GRATITUDE

Set a timer for two minutes. Then use the space below to list what you're grateful for. Let the floodgates open! List anything and everything that comes to mind. Keep writing until the timer goes off. Be as specific as possible. Notice how you feel after focusing on gratitude for two minutes straight.

What is one gratitude practice that you are committed to incorporating into your daily routine? *Examples: Keep a gratitude journal. Pick one person each day and acknowledge why I'm grateful for them. Send a "thank you" card by mail each week to a client.*

Over the next week, your challenge is to commit one random act of gratitude each day. If you need ideas, refer back to the list of suggestions at the end of this chapter. Have some fun with this! Use the space below to journal about anything you notice after completing this gratitude challenge. How does expressing gratitude affect you and those around you?

POWER #8:
CHOOSE AN ABUNDANCE MENTALITY

A few years ago, I met with a business coach to network over coffee. I have these kinds of meetings regularly. You could call them "business first dates"—kind of like speed dating, but for business. There are always the obligatory "getting to know you" questions. *Where are you from? How long have you been in business? How did you get started? What does your ideal client look like?* On this day, however, my new friend, who I had known for all of fifteen minutes, asked me an intriguing question that I had never been asked before. While I sat in a plush leather armchair in the middle of Starbucks, cupping my hands around a warm pumpkin spice latte, she turned to me and asked, "Would you rather have a deep and lasting impact on just a handful of people over the course of your life, or a widespread impact on thousands, but on a lesser level?"

Without hesitation I answered, "Both."

Judging by the look on her face, this wasn't the answer she was expecting. "Is that even possible?" she asked inquisitively, half wondering if I was being a smart ass.

I thought about it for a moment and replied, "I don't know, but why cut off the possibility of having both by saying it can't happen?"

This conversation happened early on in my business, so I hadn't even fully created my bigger vision yet. Why rule out any possibilities at this point? If my mind wouldn't at least entertain the idea that something is possible, it would certainly never happen. Maybe she did think I was being a smart ass because we never had a second "business date." I'm grateful for that conversation though because her question got me thinking bigger.

When you expand your mind with bigger and better possibilities, your mind will naturally work to come up with creative ways to make your vision happen.

Expanding the mind and entertaining the possibility of more is what I consider abundant thinking, which is the fourth pillar of creating a mindset for success.

On the opposite end of the spectrum from abundance is lack or scarcity. There's a world of difference between an abundance mentality and a scarcity mentality. If you're experiencing and expressing an **abundance mentality**, you believe there's plenty of opportunity, success, and business to go around. You don't have to stress when an opportunity isn't a fit for you because you know there's another one right around the corner. If you're experiencing and expressing a **scarcity mentality**, you believe there's a limited amount of opportunity, success, and business to go around. You believe you better protect and control your resources, your time, and your opportunities. You may even try to force the outcomes you want.

Distinguishing between these two mentalities was a big aha for me. My practice of living in an abundance mentality has had a huge, positive impact on my business and my life. As much as I would love to say I've always lived in a Kumbaya world, where I believed there was more than enough opportunity available for everyone, my inner thoughts and fears would have revealed a very different truth below the surface. Early on in business, for example, when I would see someone achieve success, I would experience an inner sense of panic. *Oh, no! That person is getting ahead. That's one less opportunity for me.* It was a view of the world completely limited by a belief that there was only so much success to go around. This scarcity mindset was completely suffocating my nudge.

Reflecting back on this time, I see that my scarcity mentality was an ugly side effect of my struggle with comparison. I feared that there was only so much success and opportunity to go around, and I stressed out any time I saw someone else's achievements. Since then, I've learned that consciously reprogramming the comparison habit is crucial to anyone's success because comparison *breeds* a scarcity mentality.

As I learned about what sets the most successful people apart, I started to notice something very different about their energy. It was so *free*. It wasn't restricted, paranoid, or overly controlling. Abundant thinking brings a sense of freedom that isn't available within the confines of scarcity. Believing that there's truly an abundance of resources and opportunity to go around means the supply will never run out. Therefore, you don't need to worry. Regardless of how successful you become, it's important to be on the lookout for scarcity thoughts to creep back in. Sometimes, once you have more to lose (or so it may seem), you'll feel an even greater urge to control and protect. That kind of thinking, however, will ultimately backfire because it focuses your mind on scarcity.

Here's a quick exercise to evaluate the abundance of your own current mindset. Ask yourself, do I ever catch myself thinking something along these lines?

All the good guys are taken.

The market is already saturated. There are too many others doing what I'm doing.

There is only so much business to go around.

If that person succeeds, there is less opportunity for me.

I don't want to introduce my potential client to that person. She may try to steal him.

As we've already established, your focus determines your results. If you focus on scarcity or the lack of opportunities and resources available to you, you're likely to see more scarcity. Focus on abundance, specifically believing that abundance is available to you, and new opportunities will open up. This includes being grateful even when something doesn't go the way you had hoped, such as when a potential client decides to hire a competitor of yours, or your business partner decides to part ways with the company. The sooner you release any disappointment over a perceived loss or missed opportunity, the faster you open yourself up to the next bigger, better opportunity with your name on it.

My biggest takeaway from this chapter:

LET'S RECAP

- Abundance starts in the mind.
- An abundance mentality is the belief that there's plenty of opportunity, success, and business to go around.
- A scarcity mentality is the belief that there's a limited amount of opportunity, success, and business to go around.

POWERHOUSE ACTION PLAN:
TAP IN TO ABUNDANCE

Identify a few areas where you notice you've been viewing life, your business, or your passion project with a scarcity mentality. Write those areas below.

Reframe the areas to view them through an abundance mindset. What new possibilities do you now see?

What could happen for you if you started cheering on those who got the opportunities you thought you wanted? What might show up in your life if you truly believed that there was an endless supply of success just waiting for you to claim your share?

PART 4: YOUR WORDS

Did you know that you have a superpower? You always have—from a very young age. You may not be using this power to its full potential, however. For most of my life, I didn't use it either. All humans possess this superpower (but few use it as designed), giving you the ability to change any unfavorable circumstance, person, or event in an instant. Coworkers annoying you? You can change that. Frustrated that no matter how much you work out, you still don't feel great in your own body? You hold the power to alter that perception too.

Before I reveal your superpower, it's important to remind you of the first ground rule we set at the beginning. For any of these principles to work, you must first take full responsibility for your experience in life. As in, 100 percent responsibility for how everything and everyone affects you, even the annoying coworker. *Blame* is the Kryptonite to your superpower. So what is this hidden power you possess? You may have already guessed that it has something to do with your words, more specifically *how* you use your words. Your superpower is the ability to change or create how you perceive and experience anything in your life simply by what you say about it.

Every conversation you have is creating something. The question is, are you creating what you *want?* In the next three lessons, I'll show you how a few simple changes in the way you use your words can dramatically impact the results you experience in your business or passion project and every other area of your life.

POWER #9:
LEVERAGE YOUR THOUGHTS AND WORDS

Your words—the things you say or even *think*—are creating the world and the people around you. Your superpower is a lot like a magic paintbrush. You speak, and your thoughts and words begin to paint the canvas of your life right before your eyes. If you don't like your current reality (aka the painting you see in front of you), you can always change the paintbrush. Change your words and thoughts, and you start to change your reality. Your thoughts and words are an extension of your focus; therefore, they reinforce whatever you have programmed into your internal GPS. Focus on, think about, and speak into existence what you *don't* want, and you inevitably see and experience more of that.

This isn't some woo-woo power of positive thinking B.S. You don't have to walk around in life being Polly Positive all the time if that's not authentically you. But when your focus goes off track (and it will; you're human), your thoughts and words have the power to recalibrate your internal GPS back to the destination you *want* to focus on. Leveraging your thoughts and words to refocus on what you want is the fastest way to reconnect with your inner superpower, especially in situations when you feel powerless. You can't always control what happens in life, but you can always control how people and circumstances affect you, which is all that matters anyway. Whenever you notice yourself suffering, look below the surface of the negative emotional experience (anger, jealousy, envy, hate, frustration, sadness, anxiety, overwhelm), and you're sure to find evidence of an unused or misused superpower. Your thoughts and words are likely reinforcing the negative emotion you are experiencing, and you can change that experience as soon as you take full responsibility for what your thoughts and words are creating.

Let's be honest, assuming responsibility for your thoughts and words is not easy. Sometimes I catch myself daydreaming about how much "easier" life would be if I could blame everything and everyone else for my complaints. And, full disclosure, sometimes I still do stay in Blameville for a day or two. In fact, sometimes I rent a hotel room and stay overnight, but I never buy real estate in Blameville. Trust me; it's not a desirable zip code to live in. Remember, blame is the Kryptonite to your superpower. I never commit to blame long term because, deep down, I *know* that I have the power to change my experience as soon as I choose to use the superpower of my words. Once you know the truth—that your words create your reality—you can't unlearn this truth.

WORDS CREATE

Like any superpower, you can use your thoughts and words for good or evil—not that you would intentionally use your superpower for evil, of course. If anything, up until now, you've probably been using your superpowers unconsciously and with mixed results, but your nudge needs you.

Few people ever fully tap into the superpower of their thoughts and words because, much like I did for most of my life, we act as if our words are *describing* the world around us instead of creating it. We think we're a casual bystander at an art gallery, observing a painting and describing its nuances. In fact, we are holding the paintbrush and placing every bit of paint on that canvas with each stroke of our brush.

Before I fully understood the power my words have in creating my reality, instead of speaking and behaving like a master artist, I spoke and acted more like an untamed toddler running around with no pants on, recklessly splattering paint on the walls, the furniture, and my own face. I carelessly threw my words around, taking no responsibility for any destruction left in the path of my language. After all, I was just describing the world around me, right? *This job is hard. My partner never listens. Life isn't fair. I never get what I want. Women are catty and competitive. Ugh. It's Monday. I hate Mondays.*

No wonder my reality often matched exactly what I described! Funny how words work.

Some of the descriptions I used for the world around me weren't even my original thoughts; I picked them up from things I heard others say and eventually accepted them as "true." I didn't realize that I had picked up someone else's paintbrush and started painting my own canvas, never questioning whether I even liked the putrid color on the brush or not.

Take, for example, the dominating conversation about the first day of the workweek, Monday. We're all *supposed* to hate Mondays, right? Isn't that some rite of passage for working in America? I definitely had a "case of the Mondays" for much of the time I worked in corporate America. By always lamenting about dreadful Mondays, I wished away one precious day of every week, 52 days out of every year. Over a lifetime, that could add up to nearly ten years of time spent "surviving" Mondays versus making a positive impact in my own and other people's lives.

To fully harness your superpower, begin by acknowledging that your words aren't describing the world around you. They are creating it. Once you accept this as true, the natural next question to ask yourself is what world *have* I been creating? In this lesson, we'll look a little closer, especially at how old language habits may be unintentionally sabotaging your progress. Most of your language patterns are exactly that—habits. And any habit can be changed over time. Often the subtlest change in vocabulary can make a huge impact on your results.

VERBAL ASSASSINS

Have you ever heard of a "swear jar"? Its purpose is to help you kick a swearing habit. Any time you cuss, you have to deposit a few bucks into the jar, thereby rewiring an old habit by causing pain in an area that's important to you (like your wallet). Cleaning up a potty mouth is one thing, but unlike curse words, some of the most detrimental words in our vocabulary today seem sweet and innocent on the surface. Deep down, though, these words are verbal assassins sabotaging your success and happiness.

I'll share four of the verbal assassins that I've had to consciously retrain. These are by no means all the murderous words in our vocabularies, but they're a great place to start bringing awareness to your own language habits. Awareness of your use of these verbal habits is just one way to access to your superpower. Maybe you'll see an opportunity to make a few changes in what you say and reap the rewards; maybe you're already masterfully using your thoughts and words to create the results you want. Either way, remember that what you're out to accomplish next isn't likely within the current mindset, language, and habits you already possess; otherwise, you would have already accomplished your goal. The answer to your next-level results lies in fine-tuning simple daily habits, and the way you use language is one of them.

How many of the four words or phrases below do you catch yourself saying regularly? No need to put money in a swear jar every time you use one of the following words and phrases (unless you want to), but take a close look at how much these four verbal assassins may be costing you in terms of results in your business and life. If your words reinforce the route programmed into your internal GPS, you're not likely to reach the destination (or your goal) with the following word choices.

I'll Try

Saying "I'll try" is the same as admitting that you might be *interested* in reaching a goal, but you're definitely not committed. There's a big difference between being interested and being committed. One is like slipping someone a wimpy handshake; the other is firm and decisive. Commitment has power. Interest does not.

For a long time, my language habits had the commitment level of a wimpy handshake. I never wanted to give my word to make a promise or a commitment because I was afraid of failing and letting others down. Saying I would "try" felt like the perfect escape. In return, "I'll try" stripped my words of all their power. If I didn't follow through on my word, I could use the excuse that I never *really* promised I would do something. But no one could count on me to follow through. Deep down, I don't even think I could count on *myself* to follow through.

I would also use "I'll try" to avoid using a different, powerful two-letter word: no. I hated telling people "no." Saying "no" didn't fit well with my people pleasing nature. I wanted to be everything to everyone, which made me miserable. Instead of just saying "no," I would "try" to manage countless open-ended commitments that I never intended to fulfill. Then I'd complain and resent the fact that I hadn't just said "no" in the first place. This pattern of saying "Yes, I'll try," instead of "no" fed my feeling of overwhelm. Consequently, no one in my life could count on me. I've found that people respect me more when I'm honest from the start and respectfully tell them "no." And "no" can be a complete sentence, with no need to justify or explain. If you're a recovering people pleaser like me, just saying "no" might sting a bit at first. But from personal experience, I'll tell you that saying "no" is much less uncomfortable than half committing to things you don't want to do.

Give your words their power back by declaring either "I will" or "I won't." Yoda said it best: "Do or do not. There is no try."

I Can't or I Don't Know How

Now that you understand the power of focus, it's probably obvious why "can't" has no place in the vocabulary of a powerhouse woman like you. Saying "I can't" is like a hall pass for your mind to stop looking for creative solutions, kick its feet up, and veg out in front of reality TV for a few days. The same goes for using the "I don't know" excuse. Telling your mind that something "can't" be done or that you "don't know how" (therefore, you probably never will) is like completely unplugging your internal GPS feature. Your mind won't even attempt to find a solution or opportunity for you.

When faced with a particularly challenging situation, if you catch yourself going to "I can't" or "I don't know how" (out of habit), but you actually are committed to finding a solution or producing a result, try rephrasing the dilemma into a question that makes your mind want to search for and find an answer, stat. Instead of thinking *I can't do that*, ask your mind, *how can I do that?* On the other hand, if, in all honesty, you find yourself using "I can't" as an excuse because you *aren't* committed to producing an actual result, try replacing "I can't" with "I won't," or even, "It's not a priority right now." Then see how that feels. At least you're being honest with yourself about the fact that you *could* find a solution if you wanted to. Admitting that something isn't a priority frees up your energy to pursue the things that are.

It's Hard

We all face challenges in life. I've definitely found myself using the "It's hard" excuse more times than I'm proud of. Any time you label something, you're now responsible for what that label creates. If you program your internal GPS for struggle, you'll usually get exactly what you ask for. Most of the time, whatever you're describing isn't actually hard; it's just new, and therefore, the task is outside your current comfort zone. Instead of calling it like it is, your mind defaults to the fastest excuse to get out of having to work for an answer.

When something feels hard, difficult, or challenging, this is what you could be saying: "This is new to me, so I don't already have the mindset, skills, or habits in place to . . . *fill in the blank with what you're out to accomplish*. The task may be uncomfortable or need to be figured out. But to give yourself power, replace the worn out "It's hard" complaint with a new mantra like, "This is new and it's easy!" In doing so, you're admitting that the situation you're faced with is new (hence, why it may initially seem challenging) while also affirming that it can be easy. This language will invite in more ease to your life and allow your mind to relax. In a relaxed state, your mind is more likely to come up with creative ideas and solutions to the challenges you face. Sometimes I even remind myself that what *really* sounds hard is ignoring what my heart and soul have wanted for so long that I stop dreaming. Ignoring a nudge is one of the most uncomfortable things you can do, even harder than the temporary discomfort of learning how to do something you've never done.

Have To

I have an amazing ability to turn something I enjoy into a total chore by inserting the two little words "have to" before it. "Have to" is like a fun vampire; it sucks all the joy out. You can pretty much guarantee that anything you are about to do will become 50 percent less fun when you add "have to" before it. Even something I really enjoy doing, like a trip to Target, suddenly sounds less appealing when preceded by "have to."

Beyond sucking the fun out of life, "have to" tends to dilute what my true priorities are and distract me from what will actually move my business forward. For example, I'll start relating to my random errands as "have to" priorities, when in truth, accomplishing these errands doesn't usually get me any closer to my goals. Like, if I don't pick up mouthwash at the grocery store today, no one will die. When I realize my "have to" list is getting longer than what I can physically accomplish in a day, I stop to ask myself, "Does this task move me closer to my highest priority goals at the moment? Does it *really* have to be done today, or can it wait?" This helps me get clear about my priorities and protect my time (something we'll talk more about in a later section).

Once I learned about the power of gratitude, how often I say I "have to" really started to become apparent to me. By saying that I "had to" do something, I was mostly creating overwhelm around a huge blessing that other people would give anything to be able to do.

To shift this verbal assassin, I started replacing "have to" with "get to." I don't *have* to go to the gym; I'm blessed with a body that is physically capable of exercise. I don't *have* to clean my house, I'm fortunate enough to have a roof over my head and more blessings within the four walls of my home than I could possibly count. Once again, gratitude changes everything. Overwhelm evaporates when I remind myself that everything is a choice. In addition, by taking responsibility for my choices, I reconnect with my power.

SPEAK LIFE

Fully harnessing your superpower starts with realizing that your thoughts and words create the world around you. You always have a choice in what you create. Inherent in the power to create with words, however, is also the power to destroy. With every syllable, we have a choice to speak life or death into the people and circumstances in our lives—not death in a physical sense, but death to opportunity, success, and happiness.

If you want to experience peace and harmony in your relationships at work and home, but you complain and speak negatively about the people in your life, you're speaking death, not life. Speaking such words directly to people and speaking about them when they are not present can both cause damage. Your words hold the same "murderous" power, regardless of who you say them to. If you want to have healthy self-confidence and a positive body image, but you insult your body with your thoughts and words, you're speaking death to confidence. If you want your business or passion project to thrive, but think and speak about what's not working, you're speaking death into your dreams. This perspective may sound a tad dramatic, but it's important to understand the full extent of the impact your words can have on yourself and on other people.

Your words can create or destroy. Choose them wisely.

My biggest takeaway from this chapter:

LET'S RECAP

- Blame is the Kryptonite to the superpower of your thoughts and words
- Your words don't describe your world, they create it.
- Language patterns are largely habitual. Like any habit, they can be changed.
- Lookout for the most common verbal assassins: "I'll try," "I can't" or "I don't know how," "It's hard," and "I have to."
- Words can create or destroy. Choose yours wisely.

POWERHOUSE ACTION PLAN:
YOUR WORDS CREATE YOUR REALITY

Your challenge for this week is to bring awareness to what you are creating with your language. **If you really believed that your words create your reality, is there anything you'd change about your habitual conversations?** *Examples: I notice that I'm complaining a lot, rather than talking about what I'm creating. When I notice this habit, I'll consciously rephrase my communication to discuss what I can do about a challenging situation, instead of just complain about it.*

Throughout the week, notice where you are using any of the following verbal assassins out of habit: *I'll try, I can't, It's hard, or I have to.* Use the space below to journal about what you notice. In what scenarios do you use one or more of these out of habit? Do you feel differently when you stop and consciously reframe the verbal assassin into something more productive?

Name one area that you notice your thoughts and words have been speaking death, not life, into the outcomes you desire. *Examples: I'm complaining a lot about a person in my life, I'm speaking and thinking negatively about my body, or I'm complaining about what isn't happening in my business.*

POWER #10:
CHANGE THE SCRIPT

Remember the inner critic we talked about earlier? The one following you around, documenting all your fears and insecurities, then playing them on repeat? I know. She's like an unwelcome party guest that you can't ask to leave. If she's going to stick around, running her mouth and eating all the hors d'oeuvres, you might as well give her some new topics of conversation. Remember, everything she says is being read straight from a script that you wrote based on made-up conclusions you've derived from past events in your life and accepted as "true." Given that you have total creative control over your inner critic's script, I think it's seriously time for a rewrite. The most crucial place to exercise your linguistic superpower is in what you say to yourself, about yourself. Just as your words have the power to create the world around you, they also have the power to create *who you are* in the world.

Changing the script all starts with two small, but very powerful words: I am.

Whatever comes after these two magic words will start to shape who you are and how the outside world sees you. The words "I am" hold tremendous power. Trouble is, most of us were never taught how to use these words consciously to move us forward in life. Many of our habitual "I am" beliefs start as automatic reactions to large and small events in our life. Those unexamined reactions then go on to repeat themselves over and over. Like any habit, if you repeat your "I am" beliefs frequently enough, in time, the belief habit sticks.

Take, for example, someone calls you a name on the playground in elementary school. You decide kids don't like you (or something similar). You may not even be conscious of the decision you just made about yourself, but at that moment, you plant the seed of a persistent "I am" belief. It could be, "I am ugly," "I am different," or "I am weird." Maybe you even have the fleeting thought, "I am not good enough." Boom! You planted the seed of negativity about yourself.

As you walk through life and collect more evidence of how "not good enough" you are, you water and fertilize the seed of this belief. You see your first crush holding hands with someone else in the hallway at school. *I'm not good enough.* You're picked last for dodgeball. *I'm not good enough.* Your parents get divorced, and you blame yourself for their break-up. *I must not be good enough.* You don't get into the college you wanted. *Not good enough.* All your friends are getting married and having kids, and you just updated your Match. com profile for the seventeenth time. *Why am I not good enough?* You look in the mirror and pinch the skin hanging over the sides of your jeans. *Definitely not good enough.*

You can see where this is going. I bet if we could slow down and consciously replay each time you repeat this subliminal, negative message in your mind, you would be appalled at how many times you've been hearing, "I'm not good enough" in a single day—or even a single hour! Multiply that number by how many years you've been on this earth, and the total number of times you hear a self-critical subliminal message becomes astronomical.

With a "not good enough" belief playing on repeat in the background, you can run into trouble as you start to pursue your nudge. If deep down you don't believe that you are enough or that you are worthy and deserving of success, then you will send people around you mixed signals. It's as if one hand is extended with your palm facing up saying "Do business with me," but the other hand is extended with the universal sign for "stop" saying, "Don't do business with me." Addressing any underlying beliefs that contradict what you are creating in the world is a vital component to bringing a nudge toward your passion project to life.

My own persistent negative internal chatter is typically a variation of "not enough." *I'm not good enough. I'm not working hard enough. I'm not pretty enough. I'll never be enough.* Until I learned that my self-talk was a *habit* and could be retrained, most of my "I am" beliefs were so ingrained in my subconscious mind that they felt like they were part of me. *I'm not good enough* was as true a statement in my subconscious mind as someone telling me that the sky is blue. My core "I am" beliefs were deeply rooted at a subconscious level, making them extremely hard to reprogram or even distinguish as *not* actually part of me.

During high school, I worked in a Pier 1 store. My favorite time of year was the holiday season. I *love* Christmas music. I'm not ashamed to admit that I start listening to it the minute Halloween is over. Okay, and maybe even one or two times before Halloween. Don't judge. During my time as a Pier 1 candle connoisseur, this awesome CD of holiday music played in a loop the entire season. Three straight months of the same thirteen songs played again and again. The first week, I loved it. By the fourth week when I had heard every song for the hundredth time, I barely even noticed the music at all. It completely faded into the background, almost like a subliminal tape being played on repeat. It wasn't until someone walking through the store commented about how much they loved (or hated) a particular song that my awareness would return, and I'd notice which tune was actually playing.

Your "I am" beliefs play in a loop in your mind very much like that holiday CD. You repeat the same things to yourself over and over and over again until they eventually seep into your subconscious, and you start to believe that is really who you are.

I'm stupid.

I'm ugly.

I'm fat.

I'm worthless.

I'm a failure.

Since many of these tracks have been playing on repeat in your mind for years, you may not even be conscious of them anymore. The words may have faded into the background, but their impact is ever present. Whether you are aware or not, these deeply rooted beliefs shape how you operate. Your core beliefs dictate what opportunities you see, and whether you choose to pursue those opportunities or not. Which is why, if you aren't currently experiencing the momentum around your goals that you would like, chances are you're operating according to an outdated belief that needs an update.

ABRACADABRA

By the way, it's still possible to succeed in life even with negative chatter running in the background. This ability is a good thing because the chatter in your head never completely goes away. Every powerhouse woman experiences negative self-talk. I've found that the bigger the game I'm playing in life, the louder my inner critic gets. Some people may even use their negative beliefs as motivation to do better, be better, and work harder. In my experience, however, trying to power through and override negative beliefs by sheer force is a recipe for burnout.

Remember, your inner critic is with you all day, every day. There is no such thing as silencing her completely. You can't outrun a negative core belief about yourself. The best way to neutralize the impact of a negative belief is to face it head-on, then evaluate whether the belief is true or not. Usually, it's not. Reframing and rewriting the inner critic's script is all about creating more ease around getting to where you want to go by rewiring your subconscious beliefs to support you, rather than undermine you.

If you remember back to our conversation about the comfort zone, we talked about how your mind at a subconscious level wants nothing to do with growth or change. Language is a powerful way to access your subconscious mind and plant seeds of belief that will align with the next level of results you want to achieve. If the mind wants certainty (and it does), you can plant the supporting evidence for your goal in language *first*, thereby lessening the resistance your mind will feel when you step out of your current comfort zone.

In the past, this is where I went wrong. I think many others do too. I always thought I had to work to become a powerful and successful woman *first*. Then, I used to believe, my internal dialogue would start to match. I had the order all backwards. If you were a magician, your "I am" belief would be less of your "ta-da!" at the end of an impressive magic trick and more like the "abracadabra!" that comes before you wow the crowd. In other words, create who you want to be in language first. Then start to think, speak, and act in alignment with the "I am" you've created.

Of course, when you first start affirming the qualities about yourself that you want to experience more of, it may feel like a lie. Your inner critic will fight the script change because your new affirmations may go against everything your inner critic has learned about you up to this point. Remember, it took repetition for the current "playlist" of negative self-talk to seep into your subconscious, so expect that it will take time and repetition to change it. Just like the old thought patterns became habit without you realizing it, before long, the new "I am" belief you've created about yourself can become a habit, too.

Whenever you notice that you've been producing the same results for a while—in your business or passion project, in your health and fitness, in your relationships—chances are there is an underlying belief reinforcing those results. If you are in a place where you feel frustrated, like you're working twice as hard but not getting anywhere, it's worthwhile to examine any underlying beliefs that may be keeping you "stuck." Rewriting the belief won't magically change your outward results in and of itself, but what it *will* do is enlist the help of your powerful subconscious mind to reach your new goals. Keep in mind you are infinitely capable of growing, changing, and learning new things. You're not stuck with any way of being or any decisions you've made about yourself. Now that you understand how powerful your words are, you can start using them to *create* who you wish to be.

HOW DO YOU WANT TO FEEL?

Answering the question, "How do I want to feel?" is a great place to start rewriting your "I am" statements and creating the woman you want to become. We typically set goals because of the *feeling* we believe that accomplishing those goals will bring. That's why I've asked you to start identifying the core feelings you want to experience about getting clear on exactly what you want. After years of working with men and women to make healthy lifestyle changes, I've learned that it's not actually the clothing size or the number on the scale that people are after, it's how they believe that size or number will make them *feel.* With any goal, it's the feeling we're really after. If you want to speed up the process of accomplishing your goals, start affirming those positive feelings *first.* You'll do an exercise around this as part of your action plan at the end of this chapter.

By affirming how you want to feel *first,* you plant the suggestion for your subconscious mind to go in search of whatever will fulfill that suggestion. Then it's your job to reinforce the feeling by asking yourself what you can do right *now* to start experiencing more of that feeling. You'll have the opportunity to start creating your list of new "I am" statements at the end of this lesson. When you do, don't go by what you think is reasonable for you to achieve. You can create any feeling you want to experience by first speaking it into existence. Consider these feelings, for example:

I am strong.

I am powerful.

I am unstoppable.

I am abundant.

I am healthy and vibrant.

Once you have identified the core feeling you want to experience, create the habit of speaking and focusing on your new "I am" phrases at least once if not multiple times each day. I repeat my "I am" statements anywhere and everywhere. In the gym, I'll use an empowering mantra to get me through a particularly difficult workout. *I am strong. I am powerful.* When I notice my energy dip mid-afternoon while powering through a writing session, I'll repeat things like *I am vibrant and energetic. I am blessed to do what I love every day.* Any time I feel disconnected from my power, chances are I've got some negative self-talk going on in the background. That's my cue to consciously replace any self-talk that isn't moving me forward with something that will.

Self-love and affirmation, just like gratitude, work best when sprinkled around like confetti.

Speaking of gratitude, another powerful way to cement these new "I am" affirmations in your mind as a habit is to pair them with your daily gratitude practice. Gratitude creates a powerful flow of positive energy in your mind. Linking an affirmation with this positive emotional energy will help it stick. Your practice could be as simple as writing five or ten items of gratitude in a journal every morning, followed by five or ten "I am" beliefs that you create. In the next lesson, we'll expand upon the idea of planting new seeds of belief in your mind, enlisting the help of your subconscious mind to create *any* results you want.

My biggest takeaway from this chapter:

LET'S RECAP

- Changing the inner critic's script all starts with two small, but very powerful words: "I am."
- Your "I am" beliefs play in a loop in your mind over and over until they eventually seep into your subconscious, and you start to believe that is really who you are.
- Neutralize the impact of a negative belief by facing it head-on and evaluating whether the belief is true or not.
- Rewriting the inner critic's script is all about creating more ease around getting to where you want to go by rewiring your subconscious beliefs to support you.

POWERHOUSE ACTION PLAN:
REWRITE YOUR INNER CRITIC'S SCRIPT

Think about your different goals and how achieving them will make you feel. Then fill in the blanks for each goal:

I want to achieve _____, because it will make me feel _____.

Maybe you want to see a certain number in your savings account because it will help you feel secure. Or maybe you want to serve a certain number of people through your business or passion project. As a result, you'll feel valued. Whatever the goal, ask yourself, "How will accomplishing this goal make me feel? These feelings will give you a head start in rewriting your "I am" statements.

Repeat this process as many times as you'd like to come up with a list of desired feelings. Turn those feelings into an "I am" statement and list them below:

Once you've identified the core feelings you want to experience, your job is to act in alignment with those feelings. This will further reinforce your new "I am" beliefs in your subconscious mind. **Ask yourself, "How could I start to experience that desired feeling now in smaller ways?"** Let's say, for example, that your goal is to feel confident. What other things can you do now that give you feelings of confidence? *Examples: Exercise and get my endorphins pumping, put on my favorite outfit, connect with a girlfriend who always builds me up.*

Jot down a few ideas below:

POWER #11:
AFFIRM YOUR DESIRES

You can also leverage your words to help you create *any* outcome you desire. We've already talked about the power of vividly imagining your goals as already accomplished. One way to supercharge this power is to add language—to affirm your desires and goals through written or spoken statements called "affirmations." In case you're not already familiar with affirmations or how they are used, let's break them down.

An affirmation is a statement of your desire or goal, which you state in present tense as though it has already been accomplished. Simply put, an affirmation uses your linguistic superpower to affirm to your subconscious mind that your goal is already being completed now; therefore, your subconscious should be on the lookout for evidence to support that truth. Stating your affirmations in the present tense is an important component for that reason. If you program your internal GPS to achieve something in the future, it will always remain in the future—kind of like a carrot dangling from a stick. As you move forward, so does the stick; you never actually close the gap between where you are now and where you want to be in the future. At the end of this lesson, I'll share some of my own go-to affirmations and give you an opportunity to create your own. I know that any conversation about the power of language is incomplete without talking about affirmations because an affirmation played a huge role in what I've achieved with my career and business today.

When I first dove into personal development almost ten years ago, I learned that affirmations are powerful language tools. At that time, I started to hear about affirmations and how they were being used by some of the most successful people in the world. I knew it couldn't hurt to give them a shot. I typed up a document with affirmations for the main areas of my life—career, relationships, health/fitness, finances, and spirituality—creating a word picture of my ideal outcome in each area and written in present tense as though I'd already achieved the goal. I printed several copies so I could keep them with me at all times. My goal was to read them no less than twice per day. Usually that ended up being first thing in the morning and the last thing before my head hit the pillow at night.

A few months passed, and I didn't necessarily notice any major changes despite diligently reading my affirmations daily. This was during the same timeframe when I realized my corporate "dream job" was not for me forever, so one of the affirmations I wrote was this: *I am so happy and fulfilled to have started a business that combines my passion for personal development with health & fitness.* I had absolutely no experience in running a business, and I didn't know exactly what it would look like, but this was the closest I could get to describing my "dream career." I wanted to be my own boss, set my own hours, and have it be socially acceptable to wear workout clothes 99 percent of my day. I wanted it to be my job to stay in the best physical shape I possibly could and use that as a platform to inspire and help others.

About six months later, while having a phone conversation with my husband (who was my long-distance fiancé at the time), he mentioned a nutrition program made by Isagenix, an Arizona-based company. He'd been using their supplements and experiencing great results. I'm typically skeptical about these types of programs. In fact, I was pretty smug because I really thought I knew my stuff when it came to fitness and nutrition. We hung up, and I immediately started researching this new "program" that he liked so much. I intended to prove why he didn't need it. In fact, I was adamant that he could get everything his body needed from whole foods alone.

In the process of this research, I ended up proving *myself* wrong. It turned out there was some pretty solid science behind this stuff he was using. Despite my best efforts to discourage Elliot from continuing with the program, much less have me join him in using it, he persisted. In fact, he wouldn't drop the subject until I at least agreed to give these products a try. It only took about three weeks of coaxing (and a little bribery) for me to give in and order the program. *Whatever it takes to get him off my back about it*, I thought. I figured I would just return it within the first month and get my money back.

As we were getting my order placed, Elliot casually added, "Oh, and there is a business with this too. Maybe we could earn a little extra money to help pay for the wedding." I didn't think much about it. He was constantly coming up with new business ideas but never really acted on them. I brushed his idea aside, figuring it was just like the others. Then my first shipment from the nutrition company arrived at my doorstep. By this point I had done some pretty in-depth research into the science behind the products and was pleasantly surprised to see how much the company's philosophy on ingredient quality and sourcing aligned with my own beliefs. Cautiously excited to give the product a try, I opened the box and started looking through the contents.

Inside, there were a few colorful brochures with happy smiling people and information about the program and the company. I started leafing through the brochures, pausing on a page that went into more detail about the financial opportunity available to those who wanted to partner with the company, share their message, and create extra income. I had never heard of this business concept before, but it made a lot of sense. I briefly glanced it over and was about to flip the page when a sentence at the bottom caught my eye. I had to do a double take because there in bold letters it read: "If you are passionate about health & wellness and personal development, you've found your home". My home? Wait a minute. This was almost word for word how my affirmation read—the one I'd been repeating twice a day for the past six months. At that moment, I was half waiting for *The Twilight Zone* music to start playing. I know I was looking for an answer, but *really*? Surely *this* couldn't be it. Still, shaking my head at the irony of it all, I thought, "Okay, maybe I should at least look into it."

The more I learned about Isagenix as a company, their values, and the network marketing industry, the more I loved all of it. This health and wellness company was everything I had been looking for and more. Fast forward almost seven years later. As a result of that company and that opportunity, I was able to more than replace my previous corporate salary while having the freedom to work from wherever I want doing something I truly love. And I do it all by helping people. I'm now living exactly the life I created with my affirmation.

Would the opportunity have presented itself anyway, even if I hadn't been reading and repeating that affirmation daily? And if the opportunity had appeared, would I have been open to it? I have no way of knowing for sure, but I don't question miracles when they occur. What I do know is that speaking my intentions into existence and *expecting* that the desired outcomes are on their way to me has served me well on more than one occasion. But even though I know from personal experience how powerful affirmations can be, at some point I stopped using them regularly. Maybe I got a little too comfortable with where I was in my business and life and didn't think I needed them anymore. It wasn't until just recently, as I was setting new goals and realizing how, in certain areas, I wasn't moving forward as quickly as I'd like, that I went back to the basics. In just a few weeks of creating my new affirmations and reading them aloud daily, I'm noticing a measurable difference in my confidence about the direction I'm going, as well as some very cool new opportunities that have presented themselves.

Now, let me be clear. By no means is any of this a shortcut for hard work.

Affirmations are not a magic genie in a bottle; your wish is not their command.

The point is to leverage your conscious mind to get your subconscious on board with where you're going. Affirmations help to tune your radar to pick up on opportunities, people, and circumstances that align with the vision you're speaking into life. They help you to take your blinders off, so you can see what's already there and act on it. But for anything to happen, you *must act*. If you don't work, affirmations won't either. My affirmation story wouldn't be the same had I not acted on the opportunity in front of me and worked to create a successful business over time.

If you are new to all of this and want some help creating affirmations of your own, I've offered a few of my favorite go-to affirmation statements below. Feel free to modify them to fit your own desires and goals. You want your affirmations to resonate with you and help you tap into the emotions and feelings of having already achieved your goals.

My body is healthy, my mind is brilliant, and my soul is tranquil.

My business is growing, expanding, and thriving.

I possess all the qualities needed to be extremely successful.

I use money wisely and am continually building my wealth.

I am aligned with the energy of abundance. Money comes to me easily through unexpected sources.

My success attracts more success.

Everything is working out perfectly in my favor.

I love and accept myself unconditionally.

I am solution-minded. I can solve any challenge that I'm faced with.

You can also add your new "I am" statements to this list. Remember, the key is to tap into the *feelings* associated with these statements. If I'm reading a new affirmation and my mind is fighting me to believe that it's possible for me, I'll reread it aloud several times until I feel my energy shift. Don't be surprised if at first you notice your inner critic saying, "No, you're not" or "No, you can't" in response to your new affirmations. Over time, you will start to reprogram this inner chatter and change the inner critic's script.

One last thing—once you start affirming the future you desire, it's important to look carefully at how well your daily actions align with that vision. For example, if you are affirming the healthy and fit body you desire, but you're still eating junk food all day long, you aren't as likely to reach your goal. You send a mixed message to your subconscious mind if your words say you want one outcome, but your actions reinforce a totally different one. This doesn't mean you have to be perfect, but the more consistently your actions align with your affirmation, the faster the results will come. And the more you affirm what you are creating through your language, the more you'll notice that the necessary actions to achieve your goal become more effortless.

If you're ready to commit (or recommit) to a daily affirmation practice, here are a few tips to help ensure you're getting the full benefit:

1. **Handwrite them.** I created my first affirmation list on my computer, so I could easily print copies; however, now I prefer to handwrite them on index cards for a few reasons. There is a powerful mind-body connection in the physical act of writing them out and then reading statements written in your own handwriting.

2. **Say them out loud, with power.** There is an energy to the spoken word. Speaking affirmations out loud engages multiple senses, which gives your affirmations even more power.

3. **Tap into the emotion.** Read the affirmation as many times as necessary until you feel the emotions associated with having that result.

4. **Once you know what you want, take action.** This is probably the most important thing to know about the power of affirmations—they only work if you do. Which is exactly why the next and final section will be dedicated to ACTION.

My biggest takeaway from this chapter:

LET'S RECAP

- An affirmation is a statement of your desire or goal, stated in present tense as though you have already accomplished it.
- Affirmations leverage your conscious mind to get your subconscious mind on board for where you're going. But for anything to happen, you must act on the desire.
- It's important to make sure that your actions align with your desired outcome. You'll send a mixed message to your subconscious mind if your words say you want one outcome, but your actions reinforce a totally different one.

POWERHOUSE ACTION PLAN:
AFFIRM YOUR DESIRES WITH LANGUAGE

Create your own affirmations below. I encourage you to handwrite them on index cards and carry them with you throughout the day. The more frequently you read them, the faster they'll start to reprogram your subconscious mind.

During your day, when are you going to commit to reading your affirmations?

PART 5: YOUR ACTIONS

Now that we've laid a foundation with the mindset and language habits that will contribute to your success, we're ready to talk about the one thing that makes the most difference when pursuing your dreams: action. You can develop a rock-solid mindset for success and be precise about creating your world through language, but if you aren't acting on the things that will move you forward, none of that mindset stuff matters. Just as you can build the most beautiful precision bicycle—designed with the best materials, painted with your favorite colors, and fully equipped to perform—the bicycle won't go anywhere until you move the pedals. Your business or passion project is the same.

Successful action boils down to one thing: habits. The goal of taking action is to solidify new habits that will naturally produce the results you desire. Once a habit is formed, it takes far less concentration and effort to perform the required action. The only difference between you and someone who currently has a result that you want is that they've created the necessary habits to support that outcome. In the final lesson, we'll talk about creating new habits by taking disciplined action and also look at a few common ways you may find yourself unintentionally sabotaging the formation of new success habits.

POWER #12:
DISCIPLINE CREATES HABIT

Discipline is sexy. Disciplined action is the pathway to creating new habits, and habits are what inevitably produce results. Now, the words "discipline" and "sexy" aren't typically used in the same sentence, but hear me out. I don't mean discipline as in punishment. (This isn't a *Fifty Shades of Grey* tangent we're going on here.) I'm talking about self-mastery. Doing what you said you would do long after the initial jolt of motivation and inspiration are gone, and having the discipline to perform the necessary actions long enough until a habit is formed. Now, what I've just described may not seem like the sexy stuff. But doing the mundane, seemingly insignificant, small things daily produces big results long term. And results *are* sexy.

If you view daily discipline as the pathway to the results you want in your business and life, discipline itself becomes sexy too. I'm talking about the little daily actions no one will ever see you take and the hard work no one will ever know about. I'm talking about the determination to keep inspiring yourself over and over again because people want and need what you have to offer. I'm talking about the willingness to keep sharing your vision, even when it seems like no one "gets it." And I'm talking about getting up early, staying up late, and rocking a messy bun three days in a row because who has time to wash and style their hair anyway? You have a vision to build.

That kind of discipline.

The tricky thing about discipline is that you rarely see the results from these incremental efforts right away. New habits take time to build, and the habit is what you're after. Deep down, I think most of us know that it's the simple daily actions repeated consistently over time that make the real difference. These are the kind of actions that Jeff Olson, an author, CEO, and successful entrepreneur, describes in his book *The Slight Edge* as "easy to do, and easy not to do." By "easy to do," he means small actions that seem insignificant in the moment and don't necessarily produce an immediate result. For example, turning down one cupcake won't result in overnight abs, but the right combination of these seemingly small healthy habits repeated over time will, without fail, produce a healthier body. Making one sales call for your business may not result in an immediate one-million-dollar annual revenue stream, but making a set number of the right kind of calls every day over the course of a year will make an incremental difference in your bottom line. These small actions are also just as easy *not* to do because there are no immediate negative repercussions either. Your business doesn't immediately go bankrupt if you don't make your calls that day. And you don't drop dead immediately after eating processed food. But if you repeat such actions (or in actions) over time . . . ? You see where I'm going with this. You'll eventually end up on the struggle bus.

When it comes to the easy-to-do actions, and the discipline to create new success habits around your business or passion project, beware of three traps: (1) negotiating with your priorities instead of doing what you committed to doing, (2) giving every activity the same priority on your to-do list, and (3) constantly checking to see if your actions are "working." Next, we'll dive a little deeper into each of these three traps to identify where they may be slowing you down.

NEGOTIATION

Once you have identified the small incremental actions that will create your desired success habits, the next step is to prioritize and schedule these daily actions just like you would schedule a hot date with your dream partner. You wouldn't cancel a hot date, would you? Then don't cancel a date with your priorities!

If you want a healthy and fit body, then schedule a gym date with your fine self. Want to write a book? Schedule a date with your book. Ready to take your business or passion project to the next level? Schedule time for the highest income-producing activities *before* you schedule any actions that can be delegated or moved to the next day's task list. Want to create a deeper spiritual experience? Then carve out time for meditation, reading, or whatever feeds your soul. Protect your scheduled time as though your goals depend on it, because they do.

I don't know about you, but I tend to get myself into trouble when I start negotiating with my priorities. Typically, I know what actions I need to take next to reach my goal. Yet whenever it comes time to *do* whatever that action is, I can find myself having an all-out tug-of-war between the action I've prioritized (supposedly) and the action I feel like doing at that moment. That pesky comfort zone beckons me to slip off my shoes and stay awhile. Then it offers me a neck massage and a glass of prosecco: *No need to make those super important phone calls that you're resisting. Just sit back and relax. You can do the calls tomorrow.* There's like a little cartoon angel on one shoulder and a little devil with a pitchfork on the other. The angel reminds me of my commitment, while the cartoon devil presents a compelling case for why my priorities can wait.

Sound familiar? You might have packed a healthy lunch and

brought it to work because "Operation Bikini Bod" is in full effect. Then you come face-to-face with the donut smorgasbord at the office and the tug-of-war ensues. Your angel, with her annoying, know-it-all tone, reminds you, "You took all that time to make a delicious kale salad for lunch. Why waste it? Just think about the swimsuit you'll be wearing on vacation in a few weeks. Remember, what you eat in private you wear in public!"

"Are you kidding me?" your cartoon devil snaps back. "Who in their right mind passes up free donuts? There are starving children in Africa who have no donuts. It would be rude not to eat one—or seven. You don't want to be ruuuuude do you?"

Game, set, match. You wake up from a carb-induced coma with powdered sugar on your forehead, wondering where it all went wrong. "Tomorrow," you think to yourself. "I'll get back on track with my diet tomorrow."

The same saga plays out in any area of your life, business, or passion project where you're out to create a new habit and produce a new result. Any time you step outside your comfort zone, you can expect the cartoon devil with all his unsolicited opinions to show up. And if you're expecting him, you can greet him at the door with a sweet smile while you give him a swift kick to the curb. Sorry, little pitchfork-wielding nuisance, my nudge is not interested in buying what you're selling.

The key to having what you want in life is to honor your priorities and commitments more often than you honor how you "feel" about them in the moment. The less you entertain the tug-of-war between your priorities and what you feel like doing, the more time and energy you'll have to create epic results in your business or passion project.

THE ONE THING

Speaking of priorities, one of the most productive actions you can take for your business is to identify the single highest priority task. Then focus on solidifying a habit around it. Settle on just one highest priority task—not that you ignore everything else, but accomplishing and creating a habit around this single, very important task should become your main focus.

I'll have you know that prioritizing just one important task is a huge deviation from how I normally operate. When I latch on to an idea or am fueled by a vision that excites me, I want to make it happen, and I mean *now*. This urgency leads me to create crazy detailed "to-do" lists and sub-lists within those lists. At times like these, I take the amount of actions I would normally produce in a week and expect myself to accomplish all those tasks in a single day. By focusing on so many moving parts all at one time, I take the focus off my initial intention.

I used to multitask like a madwoman because I thought this was how productive people operated. That is, until recently, when I learned the concept of "the one thing," an idea coined by Gary Keller, a real estate mogul, and Jay Papasan, the former editor-in-chief for HarperCollins, in their bestselling book, *The One Thing*. The principle is simple: identify the one activity that will most drive your success and prioritize that one thing until it becomes a habit. Drill down to the smallest action that, according to Keller and Papasan, ". . . if accomplished, will make everything else easier or unnecessary." Then plan your day around accomplishing that task.

When I revisited my ever-expanding to-do list with a "one thing" mentality, I realized how many tasks didn't actually help me accomplish the highest priority activity for my business—lead generation. Continuously filling my pipeline with new potential clients is the most important thing I can do for the success of my business—not organizing my office, paying bills, or cleaning out my e-mail inbox. These other activities all need to be accomplished at some point, but shouldn't take priority over my true priority, lead generation.

My first step in applying the "one thing" philosophy was to block off a certain time of the day to accomplish my highest priority activity. I decided to schedule my lead generation activities right away in the morning when I was least likely to be interrupted. I then looked at the second part of the equation, which was *what will make lead generation even easier? What action will give me the highest chance of success in completing my priority task?*

The actual "one thing" (I learned) is often hidden below the initial layers of what we may think it is. For me, what made doing my highest priority activity of lead generation easier was to identify the night before who I would be contacting during my production time the next day. Instead of starting my designated lead generation time by asking myself, "Okay, who am I going to contact today?" I had a list of names and contact information already on my desk, just waiting for me to jump right into action in the morning. That way, even if I was only able to block out thirty minutes of lead generation time for that particular day, I could be extremely productive within that time. The true "one thing" is whatever makes achieving your highest priority activity a no-brainer.

Let's apply this principle to the goal I set of waking up at 6:00 a.m. every day. At first glance, I thought that waking up early was the "one thing." As I looked closer, however, it was actually getting in bed at 9:30 p.m. to read for thirty minutes and wind down. Then turn the lights out at 10:00 sharp. This made getting up at 6:00 in the morning easier. So being in bed reading at 9:30 p.m. became my "one thing" activity, which supported my goal of waking up early.

The main goal of this "one thing" philosophy is to create small wins along the way to solidifying a habit. Just like I've said before, regardless of whether you want a successful business, a healthy and fit body, or a happy relationship, the way you get there is the same— focus on learning to become the person who naturally produces the result you desire. Take action to build the beliefs and habits consistent with the outcome, and the beliefs and habits will produce the results naturally.

The habit is what you're after.

In *The One Thing*, Keller and Papasan share that according to their research, it takes a minimum of 66 days to form a new habit. But here's the best part, once a habit has been solidified, the action associated with that habit no longer requires the same amount of attention and focus to complete that it once did. That habit becomes almost automatic. And if it's a productive habit, you'll notice that your results start to improve as a result.

If you're starting out in business, and working as a one-woman operation right now, it can be tempting to feel like you need to be the Jill-of-all-trades. You may fill multiple roles for a short time, but your business will thrive the more you can identify the highest return on investment activities and focus on creating solid habits around them. Just think about the long-term implications of working on creating one new success habit every 66 days. When you start applying the "one thing" principle to just one area of your business or passion project and focus your time and attention on that one habit until it's solidified, over the course of a year, you could conceivably create five solid success habits. That's fifty success habits per decade!

If you find yourself with an ever-expanding to-do list like I often do, pause to ask yourself, "How many of these activities are essential for me to accomplish my 'one thing'?" Any task that doesn't make the cut, you can release all guilt around not accomplishing that day.

KEEP WATERING

As you get clear about your "one thing" and consistently take action to bring your nudge and passion project to life, beware of another trap that can sabotage your progress: constantly looking back to see if your actions are "working."

In elementary school, my class planted flower seeds for a science project. We decorated little flower pots with messy designs only a mother could see beauty in. Then we filled each pot with soil and lovingly buried the tiniest seeds in the center. Little did I know how much this simple science project would teach me about business and life. I was excited to arrive at school each morning, so I could water my future plant. I imagined it growing tall and strong, just like Jack's fairytale beanstalk grew up through the clouds and into the sky. Hey, a girl can dream, right? Each day I'd hustle off the bus and into my classroom, making a beeline to the window sill. I couldn't wait for the moment when I'd see the first signs of life. Not understanding nature's timeline, I felt disheartened to find no beanstalk sprout shooting up from the soil after the first week. No progress. Nothing. Where's the fun in that? Had it not been our assignment to water the plant daily for longer than a week, I surely would've given up on my baby beanstalk by this point. This experience taught me a giant lesson in patience.

When it comes to results in my business, I do not consider myself a patient person. I want to see results *now*. Surely I'm not alone in this? It can be tempting to obsess over finding any sign that you're getting closer to your goal. You know, you start a new fitness plan, eat one salad, and check the scale every five minutes to see if you've lost weight yet. Or you send out ten messages to potential clients and spend the next hour stalking your inbox for the replies instead of moving on to your next project. It's human nature to seek validation that something is "working," even though most results worth having don't happen overnight.

But back to my baby beanstalk story. Morning after morning (for what felt like an eternity to an eight-year-old), I watered the brown soil and made sure my little flower pot was positioned in the perfect sunny spot on the classroom window sill. Oh boy, waiting for this little guy to sprout was harder than waiting all year for Santa Claus to visit! Then, one magical Tuesday morning, I walked into the classroom and saw the tiniest green bud starting to peek through. My baby beanstalk (its then official name) had come to life! I beamed with pride. I did that. My patience had paid off. I was now the proud mother of a beanstalk (otherwise known as a marigold . . . but that's beside the point).

This simple lesson in patience turned out to be valuable for me as I started my business, too. A business, much like any other living thing, has a gestation period. You must keep watering, tending to, and caring for a business or passion project before you can expect it to show signs of life or growth. That waiting period can feel like an eternity to the owner of a new or growing business. But nature teaches us that the strongest, most powerful creations often take the most time to develop. The giant sequoia tree or saguaro cactus, arguably some of the largest and strongest living organisms, take decades to reach full maturity. The strongest and longest lasting businesses often need the same kind of gestation period to mature into their full potential.

I wish I could say that every "beanstalk" from my childhood story had a happy ending. After my tiny bud started to peek through the soil, over the next few days the classroom windowsill was lined with colorful decoupage pots filled with tiny green buds . . . all but one on the end, which only had a lone flower pot with no bud. The teacher lovingly pulled the student aside and asked if he had been watering his plant daily as the rest of us had. She was searching for any logical reason that his plant hadn't sprouted. He looked up at her with tear-filled eyes, and explained, "Yes! I did! I even dug out the seed every day to see if it was growing yet!"

Very cute, but don't be that kid. Plant your seed, water it daily, adjust your approach when necessary, and trust the growth process. By constantly looking back to validate that your actions are moving your business or passion project in the right direction, you waste precious time that you could use to create your *next* brilliant idea.

My biggest takeaway from this chapter:

LET'S RECAP

- Disciplined action is the pathway to creating new habits, and habits are what inevitably produce results.
- Doing the mundane, seemingly insignificant, small actions daily produces big results long term.
- As your business grows, don't overlook the small incremental actions that got you started in the first place. Always focus on the basics.
- Where you may tend to get yourself into trouble is by negotiating with your priorities.
- The key to having what you want in life is to honor your commitments more often than you honor how you "feel" about those commitments in the moment.
- The "one thing" philosophy is to identify the one activity that will most drive your success. Then prioritize that one thing until it becomes a habit.
- One way to sabotage your progress is by constantly looking back to see if your actions are "working."

POWERHOUSE ACTION PLAN:
DISCIPLINED ACTION IS SEXY

In your business, what are the mundane little steps that, if repeated over time, will yield big results? You know, the ones that are easy to do and just as easy not to do? *Examples: making sales calls, following up with current customers, investing time in lead generation, creating content for social media, networking*

In what areas of your business, passion project, or life do you find yourself negotiating with your priorities the most? *Examples: my health and fitness, making calls for my business, publishing my next blog, networking*

What is the "one thing" for you to achieve your main business goal or the next step in your passion project right now? What's the highest priority action you must do daily to move forward?

CONCLUSION:
WHAT ARE YOU WAITING FOR ?

The nudge has a funny way of getting our attention sometimes. Now, more than ever, I'm hearing mine loud and clear. While in the process of writing this book, a friend tragically lost her daughter Amani. She was thirty-two years old—the same age as I am right now. Amani was a bright and beautiful soul working to make a difference in the world in her own unique way. I never had the chance to meet her, yet Amani has impacted my life in a powerful way. Her passing has served as a sobering reminder that we're never guaranteed a certain amount of time on this earth. Every day, every moment is a gift to be used for the greater good, *so what the hell am I waiting for? What the hell are YOU waiting for?*

So what if you and I are scared, uncomfortable, or unsure of ourselves? We must work daily to connect with our power and bring our own nudges to life, if for no other reason than because we can. There will never be a "perfect" time to get started. The circumstances of our lives will never be ideal. Remember, your nudge cares nothing about visiting you at a convenient time because it's not about you in the first place. Your nudge is 100 percent about who you will serve. So wake up every day and serve, love, add value, and then serve some more. Whenever I forget what my nudge is actually about, or whenever I catch myself getting caught up in the muck of trying to get something "right," I go back to that one simple truth—this isn't about me. And it's not about you either.

Your nudge chose you for a reason. You are the perfect person to bring it to life. You don't need to do anything to become a powerhouse woman worthy of a nudge. A powerhouse woman is who you are by design. All you have to do is get out of the way and let your beautiful, innate power shine through.

The process of writing this book has served as a humbling reminder to me that I don't have any of these concepts I've shared with you completely mastered. I never will and neither will you. There won't be a moment when all aspects of our lives are operating in complete alignment. Life is a process. It can be messy. And beautiful too.

This book is simply meant to be a set of tools. You may have some of these tools in your tool box already; others may be brand new. And some tools you've probably known about but haven't used in a while. With new awareness, you can now go back to your toolbox and pick up whatever tool you need in the moment, whenever something feels out of alignment in your business or your life. *Has gratitude completely gone out the window? Am I comparing myself to someone else? Have I been focusing on what I don't want? Am I paralyzed by fear and not taking action?*

I want to share two final thoughts on my heart as I wrap up this book for you.

First, commit to being a lifelong student of these principles—and any other helpful principles that you value. I'm including a bonus section with all my favorite resources and books. I hope you'll connect with me on social media to share your favorite resources with me, too. The journey of self-development has no end. It has taken me over six years to begin to master the principles I've shared with you here, so don't stress if you haven't mastered them all within the next six months. Expect that you'll need to go back and revisit certain lessons again and again. Whenever you reach a new level of mastery, you'll notice another area gets highlighted because it needs more work. Embrace them all, your accomplishments, and your opportunities for growth. The principles in this book will work for you if *you* are willing to do the work.

Second, don't go on the journey of self-development alone. Growth isn't designed to happen in a vacuum. You will grow faster and learn far more about yourself, if you surround yourself with others taking the same journey as you are. Create your own Powerhouse Posse book club or plug into our online community via Facebook. Just search for Powerhouse Posse and request to join the group! We are all in this together.

If you were waiting for permission to leap into your full potential, I hope you now see that you've had the permission within you all along. You have everything you need to answer the call of your nudge, build a successful business, or fulfill on any passion project your heart desires.

So, what are you waiting for?

BONUS RESOURCES

Here are my top 10 favorite business and personal growth reads. I'm always adding new titles to my personal library, so get the most up-to-date list on my website at www.lindseyschwartz.com

A Happy Pocket Full of Money by David Cameron Gikandi
Big Magic by Elizabeth Gilbert
How to Win Friends and Influence People by Dale Carnegie
Secrets of a Millionaire Mind by T. Harv Ecker
The Big Leap by Gay Hendricks
The Carpenter by Jon Gordon
The Go Giver by Bob Burg and John David Mann
The One Thing by Gary W. Keller and Jay Papasan
The Slight Edge by Jeff Olson
The Success Principles by Jack Canfield

THANK YOU

To God, my ultimate source of inspiration and confidence. I'm continuously humbled by the opportunities, character-building challenges, and ridiculously abundant blessings you've put in my life. My number one purpose on this earth is to bring you glory.

To my husband Elliot, my forever partner in crime, for relentlessly seeing me as powerful. Your belief allows me to be the biggest version of myself.

To my incredible parents, who have always been my biggest supporters and an unwavering source of love.

To my Inspire-A-Book community, for your words of encouragement, your vulnerability, and your support throughout the writing process. To Laura Bush and Julie Salisbury, for your mentorship and guidance. This project truly would not have happened without you.

To the powerhouse women in my life, there are simply too many of you to name. Whether you know it or not, you inspired this project every step of the way. Every time you asked how the book was coming along, offered an encouraging word, or shared a beautifully vulnerable moment, you reminded me why I was writing in the first place. This book is for you.

More About Lindsey

Lindsey Schwartz is an Arizona-based, Wisconsin-born, entrepreneur and big dreamer. After college, she packed up everything she owned and moved west to pursue the corporate dream, only to realize that it was not for her. She dove into personal development, searching for a way to make a living building her own dreams instead of someone else's.

At age 26, Lindsey started her first business part-time and over the next several years became an accomplished fitness athlete, full-time entrepreneur, speaker, and author. Through her coaching and programs, she has helped hundreds of individuals create lasting breakthroughs around their health and well being. She has also mentored dozens of aspiring entrepreneurs in starting businesses of their own in the network marketing industry. Lindsey is passionate about building community and believes that women are most successful when they collaborate and sincerely root for one another to win.

When she's not focused on her businesses, you'll usually find her hiking with her husband Elliot and their rescue pup, watching re-runs of Fixer Upper, or sipping prosecco with her girlfriends.

CONNECT WITH LINDSEY

Web: **lindseyschwartz.com**
Instagram: **@lovelindsfit**
Facebook: **facebook.com/lovelindsfit**
Pinterest: **pinterest.com/lovelindsfit**
LinkedIn: **linkedin.com/in/lindseymarieschwartz**

CPSIA information can be obtained
at www.ICGtesting.com
Printed in the USA
LVOW09s1136020517
532927LV00023B/1389/P